D1474824

IDAHO ROCK

IDAHO ROCK

**A Climber's Guide
To the Sandpoint Area
and Selkirk Crest**

RANDALL GREEN

**The Mountaineers
Seattle**

The Mountaineers: Organized 1906
" . . . to explore, study, preserve and enjoy
the natural beauty of the Northwest."

Published by The Mountaineers, 306 2nd Avenue West
Seattle, Washington 98119

Published simultaneously in Canada by Douglas & McIntyre, Ltd.
1615 Venables St., Vancouver, B.C. V5L 2H1

Manufactured in the United States of America

Edited by Constance V. Mersel
Cover design by Elizabeth Watson
Book design by Nick Gregoric
Maps by Rebecca Walker
Cover photo: Author Randall Green on Mainline route, Granite Point
  (Photo by Joe Bensen)

Library of Congress Cataloging in Publication Data

Green, Randall.
    Idaho Rock.

    Includes index.
    1. Rock climbing--Idaho--Sandpoint Region--Guide-
books. 2. Rock climbing--Selkirk Range--Guide-books.
3. Sandpoint Region (Idaho)--Description--Guide-books.
4. Selkirk Range--Description and travel--Guide-books.
I. Title.
GV199.42.I22S263   1987   917.96'96   87-13096
ISBN 0-89886-138-1

Contents

Foreword

Bear grass, white granite, deep clear pools of spring-fed water, Priest Lake, and solitude; the southern Selkirks have it all, and on a warm, sunny day in late July they can be the most beautiful place on earth. I almost feel like I grew up there—bucking brush, cracking differentials, and robbing the bears of huckleberries. They were the times of my youth, where every moment spent seemed like twenty and my appreciation of the high alpine meadows, granite cliffs, and insects buzzing was not quite as keen as it is now. I've traveled throughout the world during my twenty-odd years of mountaineering and I have yet to find a prettier country; still wild, yet accessible to those who are willing to break a sweat, be alone, and explore.

I've been lucky through the years to have shared the rope with some great people, but the man who took the other end more times than not was Chris Kopczynski. Chris and I have become brothers through adventure in the Selkirks. It was here that we learned the valuable lessons that would take us safely to the most remote mountain ranges in the world. Not all lessons came from climbing, though.

In our effort to avoid the inevitable backpack in, Chris and I managed to conceive some pretty good fiascos. Early in the spring of 1967, we thought we had the approach to Chimney Rock solved without the work. I had borrowed a 440 cc Scorpion snowmobile to get us up the Horton Creek road. Since there were two of us with overnight loads, Chris volunteered to ski behind the machine with our climbing rope used as the tow line. I gunned the sled up the hard snow-packed road, laughing to myself about what a great scam this was and knowing Kop was thinking the same. I eased the machine into a sharp hairpin turn that came around at 180 degrees, then put her to the wood as the turn ended.

Chris's screams never reached my ears over the noise of that brute horsepower, but the harsh jerk shook me out of my euphoria and back to reality. Suddenly I realized the rope had gone slack for 140 feet as I tore around the hairpin. The bowline knot Chris had used to tie himself to the end of the rope was inescapable; as the rope became taut it whip-cracked a

▲ *Theresa DeLorenzo Green on Ho-Di-Do,
(photo, Joe Bensen)*

frantic Kopczynski into the nearby creek bottom. Quickly I ran around the curve and jumped down the bank to untie Chris; he was doing a handstand elbow-deep in the creek. Through my laughter, I made him promise not to do the things he was threatening or I wouldn't help him out. Since his arms were nearly frozen, he reluctantly agreed to refrain from physical abuse.

Occasionally, though, I did manage to reach the "Rock" and get my licks in. Clearly, my most unforgettable "air-time" was on the South Nose route, that knife-edged windy corner that would make an eagle dizzy. Jim Spearman was comfortably belaying in the sun below the crack that led to the first bulge. I had nailed and free-climbed to a bolt, evidence of Beckey's first ascent. I yelled down to Jim that I was clipping into a bolt, believing it to be a solid placement. I always thought bolts were solid, but I've since changed my mind.

Jim hooked the belay line around his leg and retrieved his camera for a shot just as I stepped into my etrier and found myself in flight. I remember trying to figure out why I was still falling because my pins had been solid before the bolt. Finally, my guts and back told me I was coming to a halt slightly above Jim who was elevatoring towards me.

The bolt had sheared (I could have sworn Fred Beckey had epoxied it in place), and combined with Jim looking for his camera, I had taken a good eighty feet of air time before I came to a stop. I finished the pitch after reclimbing my pins and slamming in a solid Lost Arrow above the old sheared bolt.

I've got a family now—have had one since 1972. Joyce, my wife, accompanied me on a first ascent and has climbed the "Rock" several times. Eventually, my son, Jess, may want to try, but that is up to him. I am not pressing him to do so.

If I was ever to love a place, it would be the Selkirks. It's my home in the mountains, where I grew up, matured, found friends, and had the best of times. There's plenty of space in northern Idaho, so I won't be bumping into anyone. But if I do, I'll recognize you as a friend because there's a spirit in those who explore the Selkirks and that spirit will recognize a kindred soul.

John Roskelley

Acknowledgments

I would like to mention some special people who helped make this manuscript possible. Without the continual support from my wife, Theresa, and the local climbing community, I would probably have given up on this project long ago. The individual who helped me organize my original ideas into manuscript form is my good friend and old-time climbing companion, Joe Bensen. Joe was in part responsible for the preliminary editing and proofreading process. He is also responsible for most of the excellent photographs included. Rebecca Walker is the artist who illustrated all the line topos. Her patience was remarkable. She transferred my rough drawings into a professional presentation from which I think readers will benefit.

Many, many people helped recount first ascents so I could transcribe the route descriptions of the climbs I had not been on. One of those individuals who pioneered many a hard rock climb in this area was John Roskelley. Currently, John is climbing and guiding in the Himalaya. He continues to contribute to the sport at home and abroad. Dane Burns is another who has helped immensely with route information regarding the Chimney Rock area. Dane has pioneered more hard (5.11) routes there than anyone else. Detail topo information of the hard routes and route history of that area were Dane's main contributions. Also, Dane and I worked together extensively on categorizing and comparing routes to reasonably standardize ratings. Many other climbers in the Inland Northwest assisted in this task also.

I would like to thank you all. Your contribution was not to me, but to the climbing community.

Introduction

Climbing is not normally associated with northern Idaho. It is a land renowned for its crystal glacier lakes, trophy-sized trout, and mature forests. Dense forests concentrated early transportation and activity along the waterways. These lakes and rivers continue to be the focus of recreation, but the mountains surrounding this area are attracting increasing numbers of climbers.

Though quality rock climbing can be found here, it has been slow to be discovered. Chimney Rock, the best-known summit in the Selkirks, was first climbed in the 1930s by climbers visiting from the Seattle area. As several top climbers from outside the region began to draw attention to Chimney Rock, word slowly spread about the granite tower in the Idaho Panhandle.

Ed Cooper and Fred Beckey, trend setters in their own right, made several ascents of Chimney Rock by new routes before locals—climbers from the Spokane, Coeur d'Alene, Sandpoint and vicinity—began to take an interest in pioneering new lines. In the late 1950s and early 1960s Cooper and Beckey brought with them new techniques and confidence that were unknown to the locals at the time. With some of the psychological barriers removed, many Spokane climbers began to move into the forefront of Sandpoint climbing history.

The Spokane Mountaineers began to influence many young men who would practice their rock-craft skills along the Selkirk Crest, pioneering many new peaks and routes. Chris Kopczynski and John Roskelley, now well known for their Himalayan climbing achievements, made their first real rock climbs on Chimney Rock. These two in turn influenced countless numbers of younger climbers, some of whom, like Kim Momb, would develop into world-class climbers as well.

Now the town of Sandpoint has become the hub of climbing activity in the Panhandle and is supporting an increasing number of resident climbers. Located on the northwestern shore of Pend Oreille Lake, and fifty miles south of the Canadian border, Sandpoint offers easy accessibility to local practice crags and peaks along the Selkirk Crest. Now that

▲ *Author on Poster Child, Laclede Practice Rocks (photo, Joe Bensen)*   11

a local mountain shop offers climbing classes, many new climbers have been introduced to the sport. Some local climbers are responsible for the discovery and development of several practice crags. With more people participating in rock climbing and the number of new routes increasing, there is a need for a source of credible information documenting the sport's local history. Hence, a guidebook for the Sandpoint area is overdue.

The purpose of this guide is to direct climbers to the most accessible and climbable rock. Backpackers, hikers, and those interested in bagging peaks may find the access and camping information helpful. Some of the more pristine high mountain lakes and seldom-visited summits along the crest can be difficult to get to. This guide also attempts to unify old and new information about routes, standardize ratings and names, and pass on the ethics shared by the local climbing community. Still, little is known about this area by outside climbers, and the standards here are significantly lower compared to other areas around the country. Efforts to record ascents, locations, and access, are helping Sandpoint gain its due recognition as a climbing center.

This guide is not intended to be an instruction manual. If you are not experienced in the necessary skills for technical rock climbing, consult a local climbing school, climbing club, or mountaineering shop for available courses. The following section entitled Grading of Climbs describes the system this guide uses to classify difficulty of approaches and ascents. Technical climbing routes are briefly described by a written description but should be cross-referenced with the line drawings and photographs. In Part One, routes are numbered, but Part Two routes are identified with letters in order to distinguish them from the numbered pitches.

The climbing in northern Idaho is varied, interesting, and often superb, making this area worth a visit. Its uncrowded routes and beautiful vistas from the crags and mountaintops are unmatched anywhere.

An attempt has been made to present this material accurately, but inevitably errors and discrepancies will be found. I hope the information this guide contains will help readers enjoy this area as I have. Additional information concerning new routes, route histories, route descriptions, facts of interest, and any corrections or criticisms of this material will be appreciated. Direct all correspondence to: Randall Green, P.O. Box 1023, Sandpoint, Idaho, 83864.

Grading of Climbs

Several systems have been devised to indicate the difficulty and technical demands of rock climbing. Classifying climbing routes is highly subjective and may be affected by psychological and physiological factors, type of rock, and how well it protects. These variables generally do not need to be considered when hill-walking or scrambling. However, Class 5 and Class 6 (aid) climbing may have a wide range of difficulty and technical demands. The rating system used in this guide is the widely known and accepted Decimal System, developed at Tahquitz Rock in central California in the early 1950s.

The six classes of climbing are as follows:

Class 1—Trail hiking.

Class 2—Hiking over rough ground like talus and scree that may include the use of hands for stability.

Class 3—Scrambling that requires the use of hands and careful foot placement.

Class 4—Scrambling over steep and exposed terrain using a rope.

Class 5—Serious climbing demanding the use of a rope, protective hardware placements, and belays.

Class 6—Aid: Climbing that calls for the use of anything other than the rock's natural features for support or rest. This category may be subdivided by the capital letter A (denoting aid) to be followed by a numeral from 0 to 5.

A0—Placements can be used to rest on or to be pulled on for upward progress.

A1—Solid placements that can hold a fall; aid slings (etriers) are employed.

A2—Placements are more difficult to position, and they support less weight than those in the A1 category.

A3—Placements can hold a short fall only.

A4—Placements can support body weight only; long falls may occur.

A5—Enough A4 placements to risk a fifty- or sixty-foot fall.

In addition, an overall grade has been given to all routes in the form of a Roman numeral from I to VI. This rating refers to the degree of commitment needed, overall difficulty, ease of escape, and length of route. Grade I is represented by one- and two-pitch climbs that take only a few hours to complete. All of the climbs in this book are within the Grade

I–III range, needing moderate commitment and taking the average party no more than four to five hours. Examples of a climb's ratings are Fern Crack I 5.7 or Roskelley/Castle Route III 5.9/A1.

The Decimal System defines free-climbing difficulties in the Class 5 category and begins with 5.0 (easiest) and follows mathematic logic to the 5.9 grade. When climbs harder than 5.9 were established, however, an open-ended rating system was adopted. Hence 5.10 was introduced. Today, the rating scale has expanded to 5.13. Subgrades of a, b, c, and d have been added to climbs rated 5.10 and harder. These subgrades represent a finer comparison of technical difficulty than the + and − signs used in the lower grade ratings.

In cases where the ratings of routes in this guide are controversial, the upper grade has been chosen. Climbers should use discretion when they are matching the rating of a route to their abilities. They should proceed with caution until they are familiar with the rock and have planned how to protect the climb.

Injuries sustained from falls are always possible, even on routes that can be well protected. Most climbs do not have a protection grade. The well-equipped leader should therefore be able to do a particular climb with a reasonable margin of safety.

An additional rating has been added to the grades of some climbs that are difficult to protect or are relatively dangerous. The letter R means conditions are such that the leader may take a serious fall, possibly pulling out intermediate points of protection before the fall is stopped. The letter X indicates that it is possible for the leader to take a ground fall serious enough to cause injury or death.

Ethics and Environmental Considerations

These subjects have been discussed and argued at great length by most people who have participated in the sport of rock climbing. Rather than approaching the controversial issues, I will try to pass on the principles we share as a climbing community. It may be argued that no one has the right to tell you how to climb. However, the sport (like society) needs some basic rules so that our actions will not adversely affect others or the environment we use.

Many of the crags in this area have heavy vegetation; to make a free ascent possible, time and labor are needed to clean the lines. Several crags discussed in this guide are so underdeveloped as climbing areas that rock fall may endanger the climber, and first ascent parties often encounter loose blocks and rubble. For safety's sake, many routes on the low-lying crags have been cleaned by using top-rope or rappel.

Due to the nature of the rock it is common to encounter fixed protection on many routes. Bolts protect some of the face climbs and fixed pitons are maintained on several routes where other clean types of protection are impractical or unsafe. The use of fixed protection and "clean" climbing methods helps preserve routes in their original condition for future generations of climbers.

Respect the fixed points of protection that may have been left by first ascent parties. If you feel they inhibit your experience, you don't have to use them, but don't destroy or remove them. If you do use fixed protection, use caution. Natural elements may loosen placements, so test fixed points before entrusting them with your life.

The climbing areas in northern Idaho may still seem untouched to those expecting queues at the bottom of the popular routes, as are found in the overcrowded areas near large cities. There is an abundance of unclimbed rock awaiting the adventurous. Loose rock, dirty cracks, heavy vegetation, and brushy approaches may be encountered, but the excitement of climbing uncharted territory is still available to enjoy.

Many areas along the Selkirk Crest are sensitive wilderness alpine ecosystems and must be shared with their native wildlife residents. To minimize human impact, stay on established trails and use established campsites and designated fire pits whenever possible. Take extra care when using open fires. Use only dead timber, keep fires small, and burn all wood to a fine ash. Before leaving the site, make sure all fires are completely out. Dispose of human waste and waste water in holes dug well away from campsites, lakes, and streams; cover with sod or topsoil. Respect the land by packing out all personal rubbish and picking up refuse mistakenly left by others. By following these rules, visitors can preserve the area's beauty for future generations to enjoy.

Safety

Climbing involves unavoidable risks that every climber assumes. The fact that a route is described in this book is not a representation that it will be safe for you. Routes vary greatly in difficult and in the amount and kind of experience and preparation needed to enjoy them safely. Some routes may have changed or deteriorated since this book was written. Also, of course, climbing conditions can change even from day to day, due to weather and other factors. A route that is safe in good weather or for a highly conditioned, properly equipped climber, may be completely unsafe for someone else or under adverse weather conditions.

You can minimize your risks by being knowledgeable, prepared and alert. There is not space in this book for a general discussion on climbing techniques and safety, but there are a number of good books and public courses on the subject, and you should take advantage of them to increase your knowledge. Just as important, you should always be aware of your own limitations and conditions existing when and where you are climbing. If conditions are dangerous, or if you are not prepared to deal with them safely, change your plans. It is better to have wasted a few hours or days than to be the subject of a bad fall or rescue.

Helmets may be advised for the ambitious mountaineer exploring the virgin backcountry or for the safety-conscious crag climber. Most climbing areas described in this guide are free of large quantities of loose rock. However, accidents can occur. By exercising caution, you can minimize your exposure to the potential hazard of stone fall when climbing behind other parties on multipitch routes.

It is useful to know, for example, that on the West Face of Chimney Rock and around Granite Point, both popular areas, climbers may easily dislodge stones.

Climb safely and have fun!

Geology of Idaho Panhandle

Sixty to ninety million years ago the Precambrian base rocks (sandstones and mudstones) were disturbed by faulting and movement of the earth's crust. During this time, these sedimentary rocks were deformed and injected with enormous quantities of molten granite magma. This intrusion of granite forms the large Kaniksu batholith. This is the core of the Selkirks and the Cabinet Mountains, parallel mountain ranges that form the sides of the great Purcell trench. After the granite was emplaced, the northern panhandle of Idaho was split lengthwise when a narrow, north–south valley dropped on faults that run through the Kaniksu batholith. Some of the fault lines are still visible on the crest near Hunt Peak and Fault Lake.

From Sandpoint to Bonners Ferry, the highway (U.S. 95) passes through the southern part of the Purcell trench which, in the form of the Kootenai Valley, extends far north into British Columbia. To the west are the granites of the Selkirk Range and to the east the Cabinet Range. Occasionally, glacially rounded hills of granite protrude from the valley floor (i.e., Schweitzer Practice Rocks, Laclede Rocks, and Granite Point).

During the last ice age, about twelve thousand years ago, the Purcell trench held a large glacier that flowed south as far as Coeur d'Alene, where it deposited the moraine that impounds Coeur d'Alene Lake. Pend Oreille Lake fills a basin scoured and then dammed by this same glacier. This enormous river of ice was over two thousand feet deep at the dam.

The glacier stopped the flow of the Clark Fork river to form a huge lake called Glacial Lake Missoula. When the ice dam broke, the lake suddenly drained, releasing a flood with greater force and size than modern man has ever seen. Its waters scoured the floors of several western Montana valleys and spilled over much of eastern Washington into the Columbia basin.

The Selkirk Mountains were covered with ice almost entirely, and the abrasive movement of this mass sculpted the granite faces of the Selkirk Crest. The north face of Hunt Peak, the east and north faces of Gunsight Peak, the Roothaan Cirque (of which Chimney Rock is a part), the west face of Silver Dollar Peak, the east and north faces of the Twins, and the south and west faces of Harrison Peak are all examples. The list of rock faces goes on from Hunt Peak to the Canadian border.

LEGEND

Route

- - - - -	line of route
· · · · ·	approach route
↙	line of rappel
O	belay station
SB	sling belay
X	piton or bolt
T.T	tension traverse

Terrain

⌒⌒⌒	ledge
⨆⨆⨆	roof
|4"	crack and width in inches
⊐	right facing corner
⊏	left facing corner
↡	straight-in corner
||	chimney
ow	off-width
lb	lie-back
⚘	tree
⚘	bush
⚘	dead tree
*	recommended route

17

Part One
Local Practice Crags

▲ *Author on Psycho Killer, Laclede Practice Rocks (photo, Joe Bensen)*

The three practice crags described here are all very different and provide the cragmaster with a multitude of challenges and options.

The rock is a type of granite that may vary from flint-hard and sharp to soft and crumbly, but most of the rock is excellent for climbing. It can be rough in texture to provide challenging face routes like the Hornet's Nest and Chicken McNubbins at Laclede or fractured in a variety of ways to test the crack climber's skills with routes like Fern Crack at Schweitzer Rocks, Weasels Ripped My Flesh — Side 2 at the Laclede Rocks, and Mainline at Granite Point.

Mountain weather combined with the low elevation of the Sandpoint area causes a variety of temperature variations throughout the year. Laclede Rocks and Granite Point are close to the serene Pend Oreille waterways which can provide welcome relief on hot summer days and allow pleasant early-season mild temperatures as well. In contrast, the Schweitzer Rocks are more affected by mountain weather influences. Because of their diverse locations and settings these crags allow one to choose an area that is most suitable to the weather and time of year. Enjoy!

Schweitzer Practice Rocks

On Shadow Mountain near the Schweitzer Ski Area access road are some small granite outcrops. The locals refer to these crags as the Practice Rocks. Only three miles from Sandpoint, these cliffs are a popular spot for honing climbing skills because of many enjoyable routes that can be reached quickly and easily. These cliffs are generally east- and north-facing. They can be cold, damp, and infested with ticks and mosquitoes early in the year, but are a great place to escape the mid-summer heat.

The rock here is generally sound and offers climbing problems from 5.4 to 5.10. The tops of the cliffs, which are not more than ninety feet high, are accessible by scrambling around the back side (west). It is easy to top-rope most routes by utilizing natural and fixed anchors (pitons and bolts) or by placing nuts in cracks. Most routes climbed on the lead can be well protected using a standard rack of nuts, chocks, and Friends. Bolts and fixed pitons protect some climbs where other placements may be impossible.

Like many people in this area, I learned to climb at the Schweitzer Practice Rocks. An experienced friend encouraged me to keep trying when I fell, and the top-rope we used gave me the confidence to continue. At the time (mid to late 1970s), we practiced here often, usually working on problems that were harder than in climbs we were leading elsewhere. Most of us did not take this area seriously enough to consider leading climbs. However, first-ascent fever eventually swept through our little group and we began picking off the most obvious lines. Now the cliff is well developed, offering numerous enjoyable climbs of moderate difficulty.

The Practice Rocks are in the middle of a new housing development called Edelweiss Village. Climbing here has always been scrutinized by the landowners. Although a constant liability concern prevails, the owners have graciously tolerated climbers using the small cliffs for practice. The recreational value of this area is recognized by landowners and climbers alike. Camping is not permitted, however. Anyone not obeying this restriction could jeopardize future access. Visiting climbers who are un-

SCHWEITZER PRACTICE ROCKS ACCESS MAP

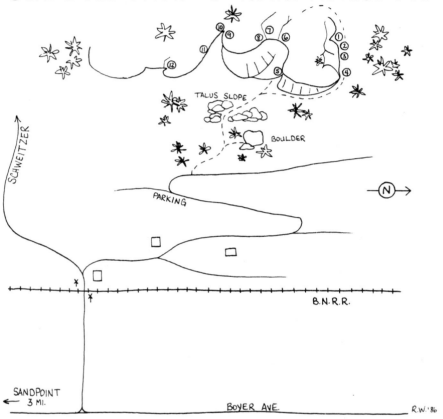

aware of the tenuous relationship should understand that if we continue to be responsible for our actions, accept and assume all risks of our sport, we may continue to climb here. It would be a tragedy to lose access to this useful training area.

Access

Access is easily obtained by traveling toward the ski area on Boyer Avenue and following the Schweitzer signs to the railroad crossing. Turn right on the first road past the tracks (head north). Cliffs are visible up the hill and west. Follow subdivision roads to the second switchback; ample parking is available here. A faint climber's access trail ascends through talus to the base of the cliffs. A well-used path ascends the back or northeast side to give one access to the top. A couple of large boulders at the base of the talus slope offer challenging problems for the soloist.

Route Descriptions

1. CAVE CRACK   I, 5.4

Left of an obvious cleft (cave) is a crack that may be climbed straight in by jamming or lie-backing to the large ledge and a short scramble to the top.

2. BATSO   I, 5.8+

Climb the face left of the cave past two bolts, and work up around overhanging blocks to a direct finish.

3. FERN CRACK   I, 5.7

A small fern growing out of a thin crack gives this route its name. An awkward lie-back leads to the top of a rock spike. Follow the crack to a sloping ledge. Continue up to ceiling blocks. After encountering a bolt and fixed pins, move left to an impossible-looking roof. Climb left around the roof and up to the tree to belay.

3a. FERN CRACK—ASTRO MONKEY ROOF VARIATION   5.10b

Directly above the plumb line of Fern Crack is a right-sloping, over-hanging off-width crack that leads to the top. A long reach is necessary to grasp a hidden hand crack which protects well with Friends. If your ape index is low, the climb may be 5.10d. Very strenuous.

4. DEFINITELY MAYBE   I, 5.9 (R)

Face climb left past a bolt to a shallow groove. Continue straight up on poor protection or follow right—sloping ramp to Fern Crack route.

5. REPTILIAN   I, 5.7

Follow the first line of weakness on the right side of the east face. Face climb corner past two fixed pins to a sloping ramp. Slither onto a ramp and continue up and right into a chimney choked with blocks.

5a. REPTILIAN—IN AND OUT VARIATION   5.8+

Scramble up sloping dirt ramp to the base of the broken blocks at the start of Shortcake. Climb up directly ten feet, then go right. Follow a crack to the Reptilian ramp (crux). From the ramp, continue up the face on clean knobs and crystals to the summit.

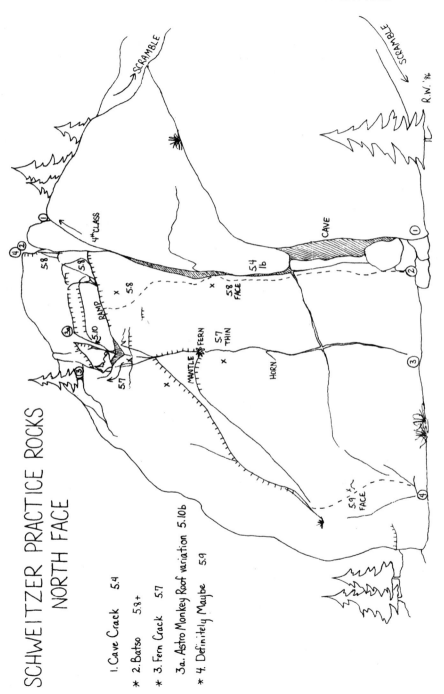

SCHWEITZER PRACTICE ROCKS
NORTH FACE

1. Cave Crack   5.4
* 2. Batso   5.8+
* 3. Fern Crack   5.7
3a. Astro Monkey Roof variation 5.10b
* 4. Definitely Maybe   5.9

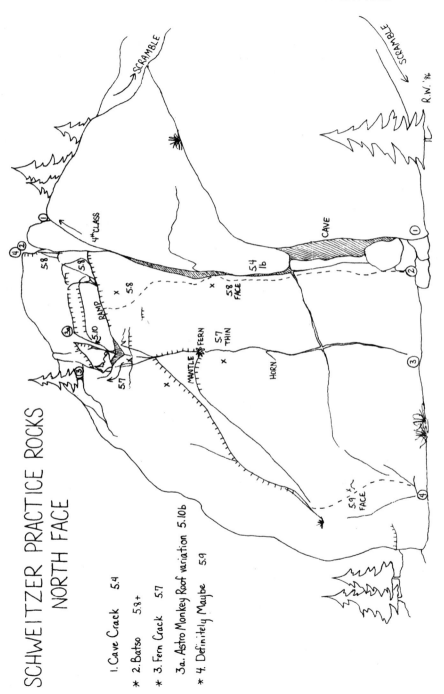

Schweitzer Practice Rocks

23

6. SHORTCAKE   I, 5.6

Scramble up the steep dirt ramp to broken blocks under a ceiling or roof, which is left of Reptilian. Traverse left out past shattered blocks into an obvious crack/chimney system. Climb to the top of the cliff. Belay in the V slot. Fixed belay anchors are in place.

7. MUSKRAT LOVE   I, 5.9 (R)

Left of Shortcake is a thin crack that splits the upper part of the cliff. Face climb directly up to it from the Shortcake belay blocks. The crack is the crux, but the face is rough and textured.

8. LACERATION   I, 5.7 (R)

Scramble left from Shortcake belay blocks and up a steep gully until the next crack system may be ascended. Follow this to a left-slanting offwidth crack with a bush in it. Continue to the top. Fixed belay anchors will be found there.

9. HO-DI-DO   I, 5.10a

Start in the gully between Laceration and Blindman's Bluff. Old white sling on bush marks the belay spot. Ascend the shattered crack system up steep rock to easier ground. This brings you to the crux at an overhanging hand crack. Continue to top of cliff and belay from top of Laceration.

9a. HO-DI-DO—EXIT STAGE RIGHT VARIATION   5.10a

An alternate finish to Ho-Di-Do. At the small roof where the overhanging hand crack goes up, follow another crack system that leads right. This line (crux) is characterized by a strenuous undercling.

10. BLINDMAN'S BLUFF   I, 5.5

At the end of the gully that splits the main cliff is a short grungy crack system. Follow the line of least resistance to the top.

10a. BLINDMAN'S BLUFF—RIGHT VARIATION   5.8

Begin at the same place as route 10 (Blindman's Bluff), but climb up steeper ground to a cleaner crack system.

11. METAMORPHOSIS   I, 5.10c (R)

Left of the Blindman's Bluff corner (gully between the two main faces) is a system of cracks and flakes that is partially hidden by trees. Undercling/lie-back the flake until it is possible to hand traverse left to an easier vertical flake. At the top of this flake, move up and right using face

SCHWEITZER PRACTICE ROCKS
EAST FACE

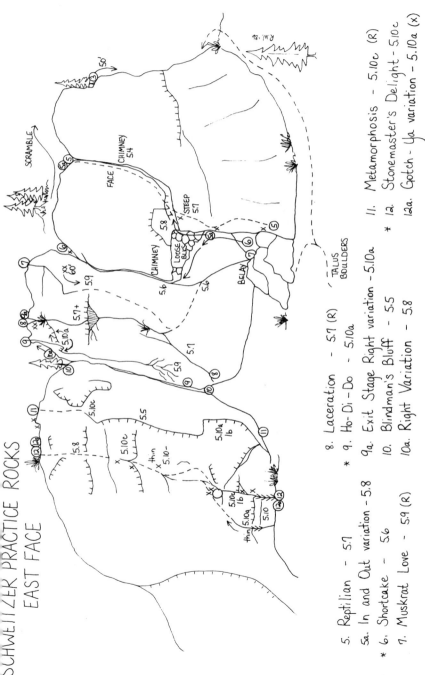

5. Reptilian - 5.9
5a. In and Out variation - 5.8
* 6. Shortcake - 5.6
7. Muskrat Love - 5.9 (R)

8. Laceration - 5.9 (R)
* 9. Ho-Di-Do - 5.10a
9a. Exit Stage Right variation - 5.10a
10. Blindman's Bluff - 5.5
10a. Right Variation - 5.8

11. Metamorphosis - 5.10c (R)
* 12. Stonemaster's Delight - 5.10c
12a. Gotch-Ya variation - 5.10a (x)

holds until it is possible to pull over another flake that forms a small roof. Face climb to the top.

12. STONEMASTER'S DELIGHT   I, 5.10c

The next major weakness left of Route 11 starts in a dihedral that is capped by a large roof. Stem the corner to the roof. A combination of tricky footwork and finger-tip lie-backing enables the climber to ascend the finger crack that splits the roof on the left side. Once past the roof (first crux), use an intermediate belay to counter the potential rope drag around the roof. Above are two more separate but well-protected cruxes with easier climbing above them.

12a. STONEMASTER'S DELIGHT—GOTCH-YA VARIATION LEFT 5.10a (X)

Begin at Route 12, traverse left following a thin undercling. Climb over a roof to a thin crack. Follow the crack past an overhang and join Route 12 (Stonemaster's Delight) again to finish.

▲ Ho-Di-Do (photo, Joe Bensen)

2
Laclede Rocks

Laclede, the small sawmill and logging community two miles away, gives this area its name. Located twelve miles west of Sandpoint on Highway 2 is a group of granite outcrops. The granite here was so close to the Pend Oreille River that the highway and railroad had to be blasted through. The best late- and early-season climbing is found here because of the southern exposure and close proximity to the river. During the hot summer months, swimming and diving in the cool, clean river near Laclede provides invigorating relief to climbers. Although this crag area is undeveloped, it offers a variety of climbs with easy access to a main highway.

Several buttresses have climbing possibilities with routes 40 feet to 90 feet long. Generally, the rock is sound; although it is rough in texture, it is covered by lichens. Most of the existing lead routes are clean and a pleasure to climb. The steeper the rock, the cleaner it is.

The Laclede Rocks have been used as a practice area for many years. Chris Kopczynski told me he frequented this spot in the mid-1960s, using pitons to practice aid climbing and rappelling techniques.

Old rappel slings and pin scars on some routes attest to the climbing style of an older generation. Now, climbers are more interested in free climbing or in using clean aid such as nuts and Friends. Several of the modern free routes in this section were old aid routes where pins were used and removed. Today, the opposite ethic exists here. Whatever pins are used are now fixed and maintained. Bolts protect face climbs and some discontinuous crack lines.

Little is known about the early history of route development in this area. An effort has been made to unearth information about the Laclede Rocks, but most information is hearsay. An apology is in order if one of the reader's routes has been left out. The appearance of the climbing history of an area sometimes stirs up memories of routes that have been long forgotten. A legitimate effort has been made to record the current progress. The local group now active may have discovered some old climbs that some readers may have established in the distant past. Anyone with addi-

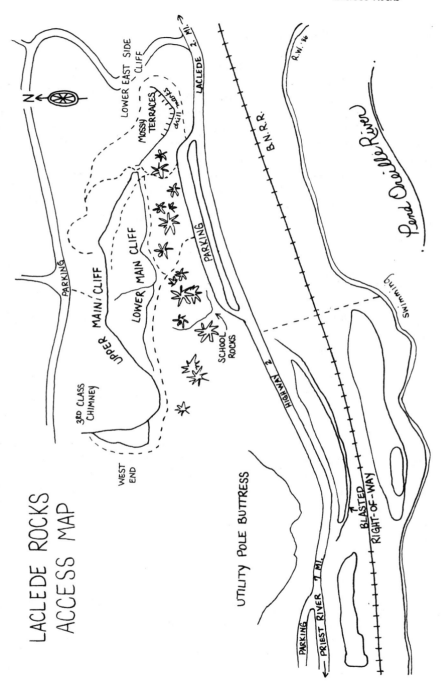

LACLEDE ROCKS
ACCESS MAP

UPPER MAIN CLIFF

LOWER MAIN CLIFF

LOWER EAST SIDE CLIFF

MOSSY TERRACES

3RD CLASS CHIMNEY

WEST END

SCHOOL ROCKS

PARKING

PARKING

LACLEDE 2. MI.

B.N.R.R.

HIGHWAY 2

UTILITY POLE BUTTRESS

BLASTED RIGHT-OF-WAY

swimming

Pend Oreille River

R.W. '86

PARKING

PRIEST RIVER 7 MI.

N

29

tional information is advised to contact the author so that it may be recorded for future reference.

Although this is one of the best practice crag areas in the northern Idaho, it is also private property. Many people here are unaccustomed to youthful, lycra-clad rock warriors assaulting sheer cliffs. To the local populace, climbers may seem to be flagrant daredevil exhibitionists from another world. Conservative attitudes still prevail throughout this area; polite diplomacy is usually the best way to solve problems. Climbers should try to avoid aggressive confrontations.

Please be thoughtful and courteous to the local residents so that the climbing community may become a respected part of northern Idaho culture. Climbing on all road-cuts is prohibited by the State Highway Department, and violators may be prosecuted. Accept this minor inconvenience so that future access will not become an issue and Laclede will be a climbing area that future generations can enjoy.

Access

Access to these cliffs is a climber's delight. All climbs are less than a ten-minute walk from the parking areas. The rocks are approximately twelve miles west of Sandpoint on Highway 2 and two miles west of Laclede. The railroad and highway cut through a portion of the cliffs to make them obvious.

One half mile east of the main climbing area is a dirt access road that ascends northwest to a bench level with and directly behind the upper main cliff.

Convenient parking is available right off the highway at the base of all the buttresses. Access trails have been improved to allow climbers to assault the brush directly toward the upper cliff. Facing north toward the major cliffs, follow a trail straight up toward their middle section. At their base, the easiest access to the top is gained by skirting the cliff to the left (west). Ascend a 30-foot third class system of chimneys and cracks to the upper bench. Another trail that starts on the eastern edge of the highway cut, identifiable by drill marks, ascends grassy and moss-covered benches to the top of the cliff.

Camping

Riley Creek campground is two miles east of the main cliffs. As you drive through Laclede, watch for a sign on the south side of the highway. Turn at the sign and head toward the mill, stay on the paved road to its end, a distance of two miles. Tenting and car camping are available throughout the summer and fall. An overnight camping fee of $7.00 per

▲Rod Gibbons on Chicken McNubbins, Laclede Practice Rocks
(photo, Gordon King)

car is charged but the restrooms equipped with hot showers and the covered picnic areas are worth it. Bring your fishing pole and swimming suit. The campground is located along the Pend Oreille River.

Route Descriptions

Lower East Side Cliff

1. **ROAD KILL   I, 5.11c (X)**

Due to the risk of falling rock and the distraction for motorists, this climb has been closed by the Highway Department. Climbing on all roadcuts is prohibited and violators may be prosecuted.

2. **JENSEN'S DIHEDRAL   I, 5.9 (R)**

This feature on the lower cliff that is the most obvious is a clean, fractured open book on the lower two-thirds of the pitch. Stem and lieback the corner to a mossy ledge. Plow through the vegetation to the top. The lower book formation is excellent.

2a. **JENSEN'S DIHEDRAL—DIRECT FINISH VARIATION   5.8**

Instead of opting for the dirty, easy finish, move left at the bush. Lie-back the flake and climb the corner system which angles slightly up and left to the top. This is a more desirable and fitting finish to a good climb.

3. **LOCK TIGHT   I, 5.10a (R)**

This climb takes a direct line up bulging rock to the upper crack system of Buried Treasure. Complex protection and face climbing characterize the lower two-thirds of the route. The upper crack is the crux. Climb past the little pine tree directly up and through the small roof. Belay at the top of the large block.

4. **BURIED TREASURE   I, 5.7**

In the middle of the lower east side cliff is a line characterized by a series of ledges and ramps that lead to a final crack system which stops at the top of a large block. Lie-back a flake until it is possible to step right onto a shelf. Face climb up and right to another shelf. Climb up to a final shelf which leads to a large ledge. Move left here and exit up the final crack to the top.

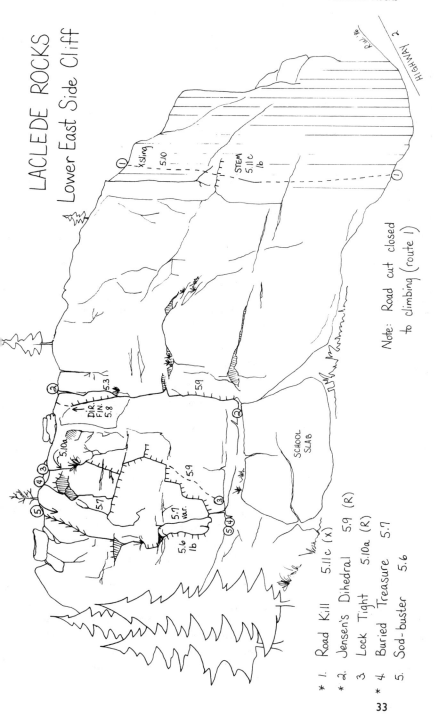

LACLEDE ROCKS
Lower East Side Cliff

Laclede Rocks

X sling
5.10
①

STEM
5.11c
1b

Dir.
FIN.
5.8

5.3

5.9

5.10a

5.7

5.9

5.7
var.

5.6
1b

SCHOOL
SLAB

Note: Road cut closed
to climbing (route 1)

HIGHWAY

* 1. Road Kill   5.11c (x)

* 2. Jensen's Dihedral 5.9 (R)

  3 Lock Tight   5.10a (R)

* 4 Buried Treasure 5.7

  5. Sod-buster   5.6

33

5. SOD-BUSTER   I, 5.6

Some recent cliff farming revealed another line left of Buried Treasure. This climb ascends a line of short cliffs to small hanging meadows and eventually finishes below the Lower East Side Cliff tree rappel station. Lie-back the same flake that starts at route 4 (Buried Treasure), then stem past a triangular roof to a ledge (meadow). Continue plowing up the next corner to another terrace and the final easy corner to the top.

Upper Main Cliff: East Side

Many top-rope protected variations are possible on the challenging knobby face that forms the right side of the main cliff. The lead routes are described below. Routes on the lower cliff average 50 feet in length; the upper cliff routes average 85 feet.

1. DRAG QUEEN   I, 5.7

On the slabs that form the right (east) side of the upper cliff are several interesting and varied face climbs. Drag Queen ascends the right side of the detached pinnacle and skirts the prominent roof to the right. Once past the roof (massive rope drag!), ascend the arete (no protection) to the top.

2. DOUBLE TROUBLE   I, 5.8 (R)

This enjoyable route begins at the lower middle section of the detached pinnacle and ascends straight up the main slab/face past a bolt. Near the top, the rock steepens but a fixed piton protects the final crux.

3. HORNET'S NEST   I, 5.8—

Stem and chimney up the wide crack formed by the left side of the detached pinnacle until it is possible to step left onto the main slab/face. Here a bolt gives security until you reach the small roof which splits the lower face. A large pocket in the underside of the roof takes large Friends well and marks the crux. Once past the roof, scramble up the easy slab above to the next bolt. Once past the bolt, exit up left near the small tree for an easier finish or assault the Double Trouble finish.

4. THE DIHEDRAL   I, 5.9—

The next major feature that cleaves the cliff left of the Hornet's Nest slab area is a shallow system of dihedrals and flakes that angles up and left. A small tree marks the top. Assault the wide flake system at the bottom or ascend directly on knobby face holds to a bolt (5.8). Climb straight up to the main flake system in the middle of the face. Two fixed pins protect the next serious section. A tricky lie-back characterizes the crux. Continue to lie-back until it is possible to step right onto a small ledge. A bolt protects the beginning of challenging, edgy face climbing straight toward the top. A variation finish may be climbed by lie-backing the flake system on the left to the top.

5. CHICKEN MCNUBBINS   I, 5.10b

Left of The Dihedral is a small, prominent roof. Start by face climbing up to the roof and lie-backing around it to the right. Once past the roof, move left up a ramp past the first bolt. Continue up on face holds (protruding nubbins). Follow the line of least resistance to the upper flake system which exits under the bolted rappel station.

6. WEASELS RIPPED MY FLESH—SIDE 2   I, 5.11c (R)

This climb follows the discontinuous crack line that splits the main face left of routes 4 (The Dihedral) and 5 (Chicken McNubbins). Strenuous jamming or lie-backing through a small overhang starts the pitch. Once through the initial difficulties the crack fades, and climbing gets progressively more technical. Thin fingertip holds and delicate footwork are necessary to pass the crux. Continue up the crack to a large cave/alcove. Jam out and over the roof by following the crack that exits straight up.

Lower Main Cliff: Center and Right

Along the lower main cliff, right of route 7 (Weasels—Side 1) and directly below route 4 (The Dihedral) is a series of prominent dihedrals or open books. The eroded and fractured bases of the three main book formations form caves and overhanging or vertical starts to climbs. The cliff here is only 40 to 50 feet high; nonetheless, several exceptional climbs exist. Combinations of climbs on the lower main cliff and upper main cliff present several two-pitch climb combinations.

7. WEASELS RIPPED MY FLESH—SIDE 1   I, 5.10d

Directly below route 6 (Weasels—Side 2) is an open book that splits the lower cliff. This fifty-foot climb starts by ascending through and around a large roof which forms an alcove near the ground. Once past the roof, continuous steep jamming is necessary until the crack fades and forms the crux. Intricate hand and foot sequences are the key to the upper easy crack. The climb finishes on the grassy bench below Weasels —Side 2.

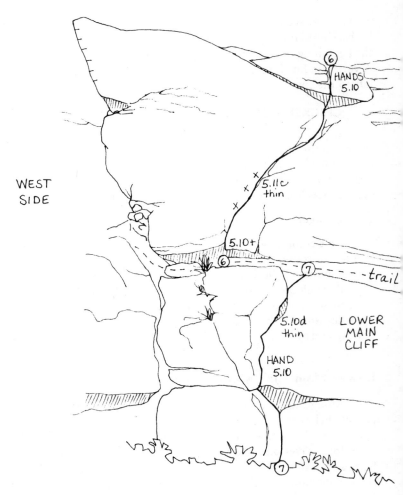

1. Drag Queen   5.7
* 2. Double Trouble   5.8 (R)
* 3. Hornet's Nest   5.8 -
* 4. The Dihedral   5.9 -
* 5. Chicken McNubbins   5.10b
* 6. Weasels Ripped My Flesh - side 2   5.11c (R)
* 7. Weasels Ripped My Flesh - side 1   5.10d

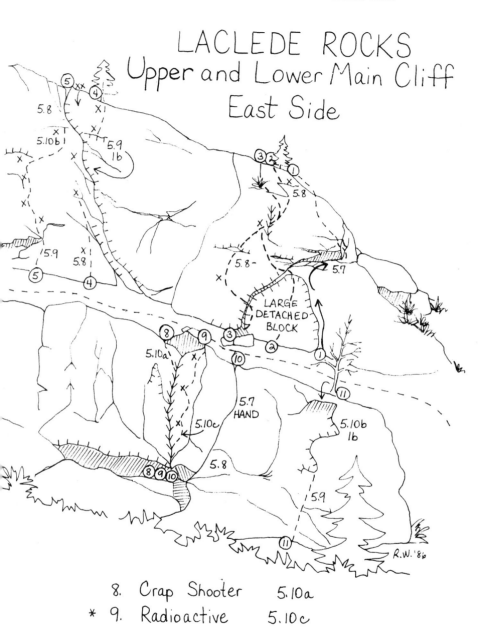

LACLEDE ROCKS
Upper and Lower Main Cliff
East Side

8. Crap Shooter   5.10a

* 9. Radioactive   5.10c

10. Hitchhiker   5.8-

* 11. Shook Me   5.10b

8.   CRAP SHOOTER   I, 5.10a (R) (roof exit)

This climb ascends a line up a large inside corner capped by a roof. A large cave undercuts the book formation, and the boulder that guards the entrance offers access to the climb. An awkward series of moves enables the climber to begin stemming the corner toward the roof. Flakes and pockets suitable for Friend placements offer reasonable protection for the interesting stemming and lie-backing necessary to exit left up near the roof. Two-thirds of the way up the book formation, an easy escape traverse is possible if the roof is too intimidating.

9.   RADIOACTIVE   I, 5.10c

The face on the right wall of route 8 (Crap Shooter) offers sharp-edged face climbing and an alternative right-side exit to the roof. Start at the same place as for Crap Shooter. Climb using face holds and exit the roof to the right.

10.   HITCHHIKER   I, 5.8–

The next dihedral formation right of route 8 (Crap Shooter) is split by a right-sloping hand crack. Traverse under an overhang to gain a grip on a sharp-edged horizontal crack. Pull up and jam the crack above.

11.   SHOOK ME   I, 5.10b

Right of route 10 (Hitchhiker) is a short steep cliff capped by a roof. The system of flakes and cracks under the roof provides access to a thin crack that splits a less steep slab above. After climbing delicate face moves, good jamming and lie-backing, albeit strenuous, lead to the lip of the roof. A long reach to the thin crack above provides escape to easier ground.

Upper Main Cliff: West Side

1.   ANOTHER ROOF   I, 5.12 (X) (top-rope)

Directly below the route 3 (March of Dimes) open book and part of the lower cliff are several overhanging lines. Another Roof is characterized by a top-rope problem that assaults three roofs directly and has an extremely difficult beginning. This line ends at a bolted rappel station that is the lower belay for March of Dimes and Poster Child (route 2).

2.   POSTER CHILD   I, 5.11c

This aesthetic face climb follows a steep and overhanging face that forms the right side of the March of Dimes (route 3) open book. A bush on the ledge at the base of the main face marks the beginning of the climb.

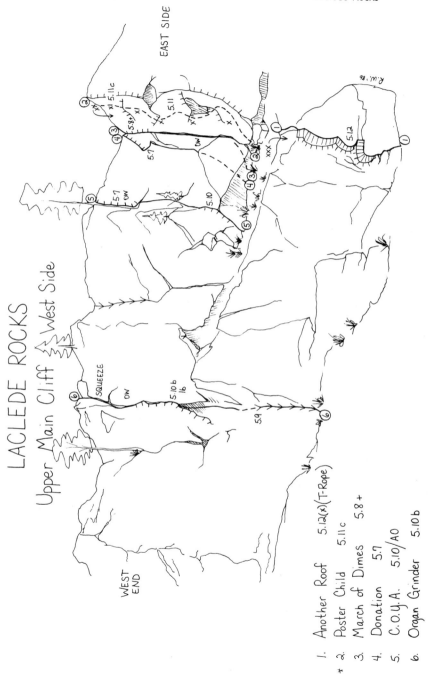

LACLEDE ROCKS

Upper Main Cliff ⩙ West Side

EAST SIDE

WEST END

1. Another Roof   5.12(x)(T-Rope)
* 2. Poster Child   5.11c
3. March of Dimes   5.8+
4. Donation   5.7
5. C.O.Y.A.   5.10/A0
6. Organ Grinder   5.10b

Follow a flake system to its end. Continue climbing on thin face holds (crux) to the top. Intricate and strenuous, Poster Child is well protected by fixed pins and bolts.

3. MARCH OF DIMES I, 5.8+

Continuing west along the cliff, the next major corner forms a large open book. Get to this book by scrambling left along the bench below Dihedral (route 4, east side). A low-angle, off-width crack starts the pitch that follows the corner of the book. As the crack narrows, it becomes steeper and easier to protect. The crack closes down to finger and hand size as the corner gets slightly steeper and more overhanging at the top.

4. DONATION I, 5.7

In the March of Dimes (route 3) open book is a detached flake with a crack behind that offers an easier finish to the March of Dimes. Begin the variation in the same wide crack. When the crack begins to narrow, move left to a flake that continues to the top of the cliff just left of the March of Dimes finish.

5. C.O.Y.A. (CRIPPLER OF YOUNG ADULTS) I, 5.10/A0

Left of the March of Dimes (route 3) open book is an obvious crack that splits the cliff. Several good-sized trees mark the upper section of the climb. Begin by jamming out of an overhang (crux) into an awkward crack that gives way to an easier crack above.

6. ORGAN GRINDER I, 5.10b

The upper section of this climb has yellow lichen on the rock, which is split by a wide crack. The lower access trail leads to the base of a shallow open book. Follow this corner to a large alcove with a roof split by a hand crack. Chimney out and jam up to gain the upper wide crack (crux). The squeeze slot above offers a rest before the final grunt to the top.

Upper Main Cliff: West End

1. ABOUT FACE I, 5.10b (R)

On the west end of the upper cliff is a beautiful line that begins as a steep crack (crux), then fades into challenging edgy face climbing. Ascend the lower crack past a tricky hand sequence followed by some long reaches to buckets, which land the climber on a spacious ledge for a rest before attempting the delicate face climbing above.

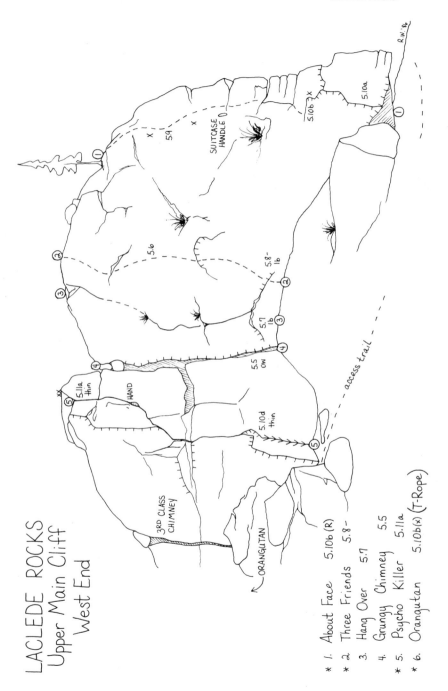

LACLEDE ROCKS
Upper Main Cliff
West End

* 1. About Face   5.10b (R)
* 2. Three Friends   5.8−
  3. Hang Over   5.7
  4. Grungy Chimney   5.5
* 5. Psycho Killer   5.11a
* 6. Orangutan   5.10b(x) (T-Rope)

2. THREE FRIENDS   I, 5.8–

Left of route 1 (About Face) and right of route 3 (Hang-Over) is a short climb beginning on top of terrace blocks at the west end. The hardest moves are right off the ground. Lie-back and face climb directly to the top.

3. HANG-OVER   I, 5.7

Between route 4 (Grungy Chimney) and route 1 (About Face), a few systems of cracks and ramps provide climbing possibilities. Hang-over follows the left system. A lie-back flake starts the climb. Once past the flake, easy but interesting climbing leads to the top. Several variations may be done on the upper portion.

4. GRUNGY CHIMNEY   I, 5.5

This aptly named cleft marks an open book formation. The cool dark depths of the crack/chimney contain a layer of moss and lichens. A short strenuous off-width starts the pitch. After a short struggle, an alcove will be encountered. Chimney or stem to the top.

5. PSYCHO KILLER   I, 5.11a

The blocky formation left of route 4 (Grungy Chimney) has a zig-zaglike crack that splits it to the top. The bottom of this crack starts in a small dihedral corner. Follow the thin crack up to a roof for a brief rest. Traverse out right and around an outside corner until it is possible to ascend a vertical crack to the top. This route is continuously overhanging and is strenuous, but it is fun to climb.

6. ORANGUTAN   I, 5.10b (X) (top-rope)

Just past the third-class chimney (left, or north) is a short steep face capped by a roof. This route provides an excellent boulder or top-rope challenge.

Utility Pole Buttress

I. NEW SENSATIONS   I, 5.8 or 5.9 VAR. FINISH RIGHT

This climb is west of the main cliffs on a small buttress called the Utility Pole Buttress, so named because of old cement foundations for power poles, which have been removed. The main wall, which faces west, is split by an obvious crack. Walk close to the cliff to avoid brush and gain access to a short off-width to fist-size crack. The crack narrows in a short distance, and a sloping ledge crosses the cliff. Continue on up until the crack fades into a small corner. Stem corner or move right to follow a

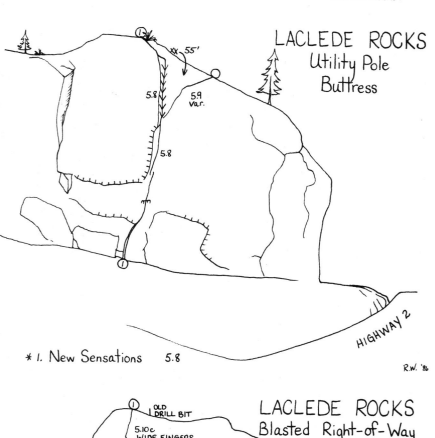

LACLEDE ROCKS
Utility Pole Buttress

XX 55'

5.8

5.9 var.

5.8

HIGHWAY 2

* 1. New Sensations   5.8

R.W. '86

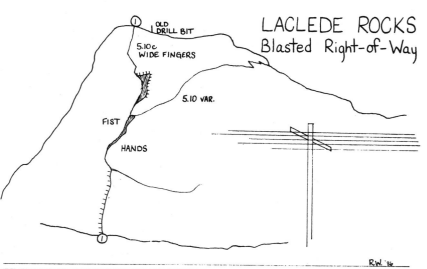

LACLEDE ROCKS
Blasted Right-of-Way

OLD DRILL BIT

5.10c WIDE FINGERS

5.10 VAR.

FIST

HANDS

R.W. '86

*1. Railyard Blues — 5.10c

TRACKS

slanting finger crack up to the top. The slanting finger crack is more difficult, but easier to protect.

Blasted Right-of-Way

I.   RAILYARD BLUES   I, 5.10c

Where the railroad blasted a right-of-way through a solid dome of granite, a manmade crack split the north side of the cut. A tree stump marks the beginning. Do not be alarmed about the adjoining wires that the railroad uses for sensing devices; no danger of high voltage exists. (If rocks should fall onto the tracks and sever a wire, the devices send a signal that alerts the maintenance crews.) Face climb up until it is possible to move left and up into the crack system that angles right, then exits straight up at the top. Be careful to not get shaken off the climb by passing freight trains (usually less than two a day).

3
Granite Point Area—
Pend Oreille Lake

The seldom-visited southeastern shore of Pend Oreille (Pond-eray) Lake is formed by a group of steep-sided mountains called the Green Monarchs. The only year-round residents there are a group of mountain goats frequently seen grazing on the steep northern slopes of the peaks. Near the west end of the Monarchs is a small fishing resort known as Kilroy Bay. This small community sports a marina, a restaurant, and a small population of summer fishing fanatics.

Southwest of Kilroy Bay, a group of granite buttresses and cliffs extends to Granite Point. Here, several steep cliffs rise directly out of the crystal waters of the lake and offer limitless climbing potential in an unusual location.

Until the late 1970s, Granite Point was virtually unknown to climbers as only fishing boats and sailboats had ventured near the cliffs. Terry Jensen, a local attorney who frequented this area often in his sailboat, was the first to recognize the area's climbing potential. He eventually convinced other experienced climbers to visit the area, assuring them that even if the climbing was not any good, the swimming and diving were excellent. The climbing, however, turned out to be exciting and challenging, and the setting was unique. Excited, the group returned often to their secret spot. Only a few moderately difficult climbs had been led, and one notable climb, Mainline, had been attempted on a top-rope. Finally, the word got out. More climbers have begun to explore the area and unearth some real treasures there.

Some climbs begin at the water's edge (Little Wall), while others ascend larger cliffs a short hike up from the shore (Troll Tower and Sunset Buttress, or Big Wall). New route possibilities are limitless and the climbs described here are a very small representation of the area's potential. Most established routes are one pitch in length. Near the base of all climbs are several small coves for convenient moorage. Pitons may be needed to tie your boat off the rocks.

The rock is granite and most crack climbs protect well with a standard rack of nuts, chocks, and Friends. Some routes in the Sunset Buttress, or

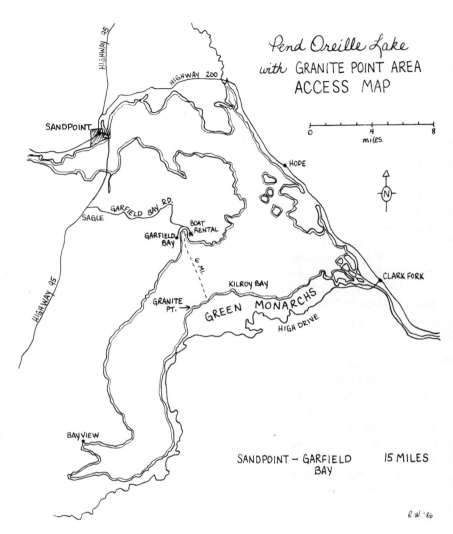

Big Wall, area have received few ascents, so loose rock may be encountered.

Access

Access is best obtained by boat unless one wishes to bushwhack for miles from the High Drive road. Boats may be rented at the Captain's Table Restaurant and Marina located on the eastern side of Garfield Bay. Garfield Bay is about fifteen miles from Sandpoint via the Garfield Bay

▲Author on Mainline, Granite Point (photo, Joe Bensen)   47

Granite Point and Pend Oreille Lake (photo, Joe Bensen)

Little Wall or Flying Squirrel Buttress, Granite Point ▶
(photo, Joe Bensen)

road. Once there, a convenient park on the north side of the bay has restrooms, picnic tables, launch ramps, and docks. It is approximately six miles from the boat launch to Granite Point.

Camping

No established campsites exist. All adjacent land suitable for camping is private, and permission should be obtained from the owner before any site is used. If your boat is appropriate for overnight outings, it may be the best option.

Route Descriptions

Little Wall (Flying Squirrel Buttress)

1.   WATERLINE   I, 5.8

On the left side of the cliff, at water level, are two square, flat-topped blocks. This line starts at the blocks and follows a left-sloping crack past a large block and then continues a short distance above to an obvious ledge belay. Scramble up easy blocks and slabs to the summit.

2.   MAINLINE   I, 5.10d

Directly at the center of the cliff and to the right of route 1 (Waterline) is a route that has a series of blocky roofs at mid-height, but has clean cracks to follow. Belay at the water's edge, face climb left to a flake/ledge system; this gives you access to a series of overhanging blocks. Climb up good cracks, 1 to 1¾ inches wide, that offer excellent protection possibilities.

3.   BEELINE   I, 5.5

To the right of route 2 (Mainline) is a left-sloping ramp. Beeline follows this line to the top of the cliff. Ascend a left-sloping crack system past easy ledges toward a large pine tree at the top.

3a.   BEELINE—110 DEGREES VARIATION   5.10a

This climb follows a connecting crack system from Beeline to Shoreline. Follow Beeline up to a bush until it is possible to move to the right and ascend a steep, clean right-sloping crack up to the notch at the top of route 4 (Shoreline).

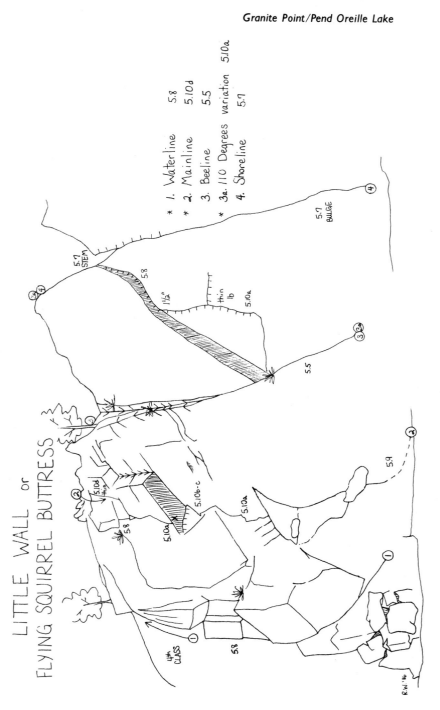

LITTLE WALL or
FLYING SQUIRREL BUTTRESS

* 1. Waterline   5.8
* 2. Mainline   5.10d
* 3. Beeline   5.5
* 3a. 110 Degrees variation 5.10a
4. Shoreline   5.7

51

4. SHORELINE   I, 5.7

On the far right side of the cliff is a moderate climb that ascends a broken line of cracks and blocks to a prominent notch on the top. Scramble up the bank to a slightly left-sloping crack system. Follow line to the notch, then stem and jam past steep blocks to the top.

Descent

Rappel slings will be found at the top of Mainline. Rappel the main face of the cliff, 90 feet to the water or boat. An alternative is to walk down the east side and descend a brushy gully.

Troll Tower (Not Shown)

I.   OGRE OFF-WIDTH   I, 5.9 (R)

A short distance down the shore (south) is another large buttress that starts at the water line. Continue past this until you can see two distinct towers of rock up the hill in the timber. Troll Tower is on the left and is split by an obvious wide crack. Scramble a couple hundred yards up through brush and timber to the base of the climb. A persistent struggle is needed to reach the first roof. A #1 slider nut is handy to protect the exposed moves past the roof and up to the upper part of the crack. Pass moss-covered rock ramps and belay at the top. Descend by walking down the north side of the tower.

Foreboding Buttress

I.   FEAR AND LOATHING   II, 5.8

This three-pitch climb will continue to be very dangerous until the large loose block at the top of the first pitch is removed. Past Pine Cove is a little snug harbor for your boat. Scramble up the bank to the base of the climb. Be careful not to dislodge rocks, as they may tumble down and sink your boat. Good route-finding skills are necessary to follow the line of least resistance. Natural shelves and ledges appear at convenient times for belays. Descend by two double rope rappels from the summit.

Big Wall (Sunset Buttress)

I.   AID CRACK   I, AI

Left of route 2 (Fingerling) is a thin crack that ascends the wall to the same belay/rappel stance. This is a good practice aid climb.

FOREBODING BUTTRESS

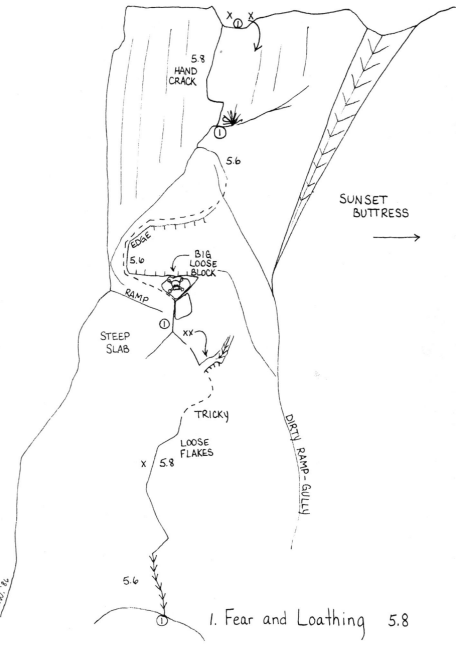

SUNSET
BUTTRESS

→

5.8
HAND
CRACK

5.6

EDGE

5.6

BIG
LOOSE
BLOCK

RAMP

STEEP
SLAB

xx

TRICKY

LOOSE
FLAKES

x 5.8

DIRTY RAMP-GULLY

5.6

R.W. '86

1. Fear and Loathing   5.8

▲ Big Wall, Granite Point (photo, Joe Bensen)

BIG WALL/SUNSET BUTTRESS

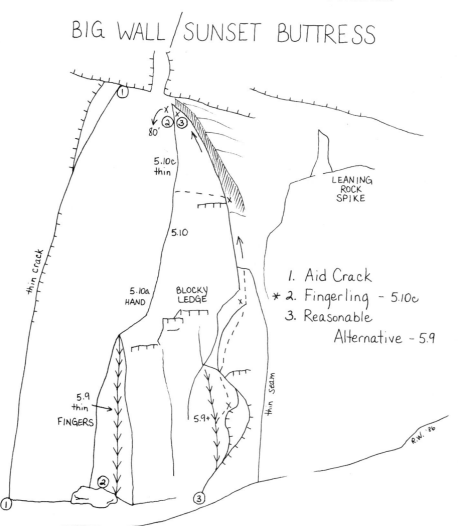

80'

5.10c
thin

5.10

LEANING
ROCK
SPIKE

5.10a
HAND

BLOCKY
LEDGE

thin crack

1. Aid Crack
* 2. Fingerling – 5.10c
3. Reasonable
         Alternative – 5.9

5.9
thin
FINGERS

5.9+

thin seam

R.W. '86

2. FINGERLING   I, 5.10c

Uphill from the Foreboding Buttress and in the middle of the Big Wall is a fractured area that has two parallel cracks ascending from a large broken alcove. The crack on the right follows a plumb line until the crack narrows to thin fingers. Here a difficult hand traverse allows escape to a sloping ramp that continues to the top of the cracks. Alternatively, continue straight up on fingertip jams to a hanging belay/rappel station, eighty feet.

3.   **REASONABLE ALTERNATIVE   I, 5.9**

Uphill and right of route 2 (Fingerling) is a scallop-shaped dihedral. Stem up corner until it is possible to face climb right to a fixed pin near the arete. Continue up steep rock to the top of a small pillar. From here it is possible to ascend a steep ramp to the Fingerling rappel station.

4.   **BOMBAY CHIMNEY 101   I, 5.7**
     (Not Shown)

Several other smaller cliffs and buttresses rise uphill from the Big Wall. A large overhang is split by an obvious bombay-type cleft. It is best to approach from above and rappel into the bowels of the chimney. This allows the climber to avoid unprotectable rotten rock below. Once at the chimney's base it is easier to climb than it looks.

Part Two
Selkirk Crest: Hunt Peak to Harrison Peak

▲ Canary Legs, East Face, Chimney Rock (photo, Joe Bensen)   57

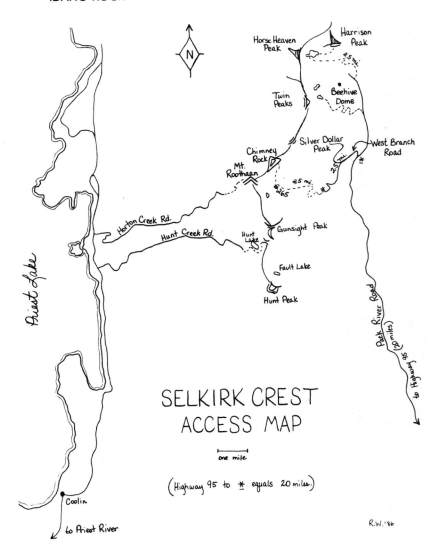

SELKIRK CREST
ACCESS MAP

one mile

(Highway 95 to * equals 20 miles.)

R.W. '86

Approximately twenty miles northwest of Sandpoint, Idaho, and directly east of Priest Lake is a range of mountains called the Selkirks. The range splits off the continental divide farther north in British Columbia, and the southern end extends into the northern Idaho panhandle.

The summit ridge that divides the main watersheds is known as the "Crest." Priest Lake on the west side and Pack River on the east side collect the run-off and eventually deposit their loads into the Pend Oreille waterway. Farther north between Sandpoint and Bonners Ferry, a small divide splits the eastern watershed from Harrison Peak north; the watershed on this side flows into the Kootenay River.

Most of the Selkirks are heavily timbered with stands of larch, fir, pine, and cedar trees, but subtle differences occur in the vegetation and the appearance of the landscape as the altitude increases toward the Crest. Although not as high as the main Rocky Mountain chain, the summits along this divide offer an open alpine environment similar to that found at higher elevations. Open bear grass slopes are littered with granite boulder fields and decorated with ornamental alpine firs, left twisted and stunted from harsh weather. Most peaks along the Crest have gentle slopes rising to their summits, but closer inspection will reveal steep faces of granite exposed by glaciation. These steep cirques characterize the north, east, and west faces of most peaks.

Early exploration of this area was limited because access was difficult. Only Indians, rugged fur traders, and mining and timber prospectors ventured into this remote wilderness. Few frequented the mountain summits except for hunters, prospectors, or geological surveyors. During the early 1900s, tough men began using equipment to build roads into the backcountry around Sandpoint. Exploration of the forested backcountry in the Selkirks was supported by the large companies that harvested timber to supply a growing demand for wood products. Now, access to this area has become practical and possible.

Not until the 1930s was anyone interested in ascending the remote rock summits for sport. Visible from Priest Lake, Chimney Rock became the first target for mountaineers. This solitary summit is the only area along the Crest where climbing history has been recorded. A crude summit register documented the first ascent and set a precedent for future ascents. Since most of the peaks in the Selkirks can be ascended by moderate hikes or easy scrambles, no documented history of first ascents is available. Only vague route descriptions and old tales exist in a word-of-mouth history for most of this area.

Until now, the best way to get backcountry information pertaining to access and climbing routes was to talk with some of the early pioneer climbers who still live in the area. John Boothe, now residing in Spokane, Washington, explored the Chimney Rock area from the Priest Lake side in the 1930s and 1940s. Neil McAvoy, who now lives in Kellogg, Idaho, made extensive trips to many summits along the Crest in the 1950s and 1960s. Bill Fix, the Librarian for the Spokane Mountaineers, currently resides in Spokane. He made several technical ascents in the Selkirks during the 1950s and 1960s, also. Bill was partially responsible for introducing rock climbing to several young members of the Spokane Mountaineers who became world-class climbers in the 1970s and 1980s. Russell Keene, a

Sandpoint resident, continues to explore the north Idaho backcountry summer and winter. Russ has lived in this area for over sixty years and is a virtual walking library of backcountry lore.

The northern latitude and moderately low elevations of this area are cause for an interesting mixture of climate. Extremes are not uncommon. The climbing season here is typical of most mountainous regions in the continental United States. Weather may be fair enough to climb as early as April or May, but deep winter snowpacks last beyond that time and usually limit access until July. July and August are the driest months. An Indian-summer September and October can be very pleasant in the high country also. However, it is wise to be prepared for a variety of conditions throughout the climbing season. Temperatures may vary from freezing to ninety degrees Fahrenheit, and summer thunderstorms that include lightning and snow are common.

Karl Birkinkamp on ▲
Chimney Rock (photo, Joe Bensen)

Glaciation has exposed some sound granite that provides an endless playground for mountaineers. Ed Cooper was once quoted as saying "the climbs in this region are a pleasant compromise between high-country alpine climbs and low-country rock climbs". The Selkirks offer innumerable climbing possibilities, and many new routes await the adventurous pioneer.

The Sundance Fire

The appearance of the Crest area was altered drastically by the Sundance Fire in the summer of 1967. The magnitude of this fire, which was started by lightning, resulted from a combination of conditions that seldom occur simultaneously: a prolonged dry period, persistent high temperatures, sustained winds during the fire run, and an uncontrolled four-mile fire front.

In nine hours this fire traveled sixteen miles, engulfed more than fifty thousand acres and snapped and toppled hundreds of trees. The fire engulfed Jeru Peak (6394 feet) and Hunt Peak (7038 feet) and skirted south of Gunsight Peak. It crossed the Pack River and burned off the west side of Roman Nose Peak. The convection column reached a height of more than 25,000 feet and the smoke column was four to six miles wide.

During the fire's main run, it became impossible to control its advance, so fire-fighting crews were ordered to retreat. At many locations fire-fighters became surrounded by the fire; some took refuge in streams, but several lost their lives when flames engulfed them. Turbulent winds created by indrafts up and down the Pack River helped stall the fire temporarily until it was finally contained and burned itself out. The Sundance Fire is a grim reminder of nature's harsh ways.

Maps

Suggested are 7.5-minute quads: Mount Roothaan and the Wigwams. These may be obtained in the town of Sandpoint or from U.S. Geological Survey, Branch Distribution/Central Region, Box 25286, Denver, Colorado, 80225.

The Forest Service also sells maps of the Kanksu National Forest at their District Ranger Office on the Dover Highway in Sandpoint, Idaho.

4
Hunt Peak
7038 ft. (2145 m)

Map: USGS Mt. Roothaan Quad
7.5 minute series

If you travel north along the Selkirk Crest, Hunt Peak is the first peak that demands technical climbing. The north face is steep and broken, rising directly above the pristine Fault Lake. Seldom visited since the old fire lookout was torn down, the summit is easily attainable from three main ridge lines.

The northwest ridge forms the backbone of the crest ridge that continues past Gunsight Pass and on to Gunsight Peak. A scramble up talus blocks and around blocky gendarmes, this aesthetic ridge line affords views of the Sundance Burn and the surrounding panorama.

The east ridge separates the drainage from Fault Lake and McCormick Lake, both of which feed McCormick Creek. The best access for this scramble is from the Fault Lake trail #59, from the Pack River, or the east side of the crest.

The southern ridge of Hunt Peak is of little interest to climbers. It is gentle and covered with bear grass extending southeast to the round summit of Jeru Peak.

Access

No maintained trails exist near this peak. However, horse packers keep a rough trail open to Fault Lake from the Pack River side. Approach this trail (#59) via the Pack River road to McCormick Creek (unmarked). Follow the trail across small drainages, Gunsight Creek and Deerslide Creek. You will wander upward through the old Sundance burn to Fault Lake, which is at the base of the north face.

Reasonable access to the north ridge may be obtained via Hunt Lake from the Priest Lake side. From Hunt Lake ascend to Gunsight Pass, which is the major notch in the ridge behind the lake. From the top of

Gunsight Pass travel south cross country along the crest to the north ridge of Hunt Peak. This is a very scenic route.

North Face

The steep, broken north face offers several technical climbing possibilities. However, to date there is no record of any ascents.

5
Gunsight Peak
7352 ft. (2240 m)

Map: USGS Mt. Roothaan Quad 7.5 minute series

Gunsight Peak, the highest of the Crest peaks included in this guide, has two faces that are large and demand respect from the casual mountaineer. Two summits with a notch between gives the mountain an open gunsight appearance when viewed from the east. The northern, and true, summit may be attained by two scramble routes. The north face shadows Idaho's last remaining permanent snowfield, which is embraced by the arms of Gunsight's northern cirque. The left arm or northwest ridge is the Crest divide and extends to Mount Roothaan. Early ascent parties approached the north face from these gentle bear grass-covered slopes of Mount Roothaan's southern flanks. The right arm is known as McCormick Ridge and separates Deerslide Creek from the Chimney Creek drainage and extends to the Pack River in the east.

East Face

Approach by driving the Priest Lake, east shore road, and Hunt Creek Road to the Hunt Lake trailhead. Hike from there to Hunt Lake and Gunsight Pass (the saddle south of the south summit of Gunsight peak), then traverse the southeastern flank of Gunsight to a small basin with an ancient glacial tarn. Good camping and ample water are available here. An alternative approach is to cut cross-country from the Fault Lake trail #59 up the Deerslide Creek drainage.

Route Description

A. WINCHESTER   III, 5.8+

Currently this is the only fifth-class climb on the east face, which is more than 500 feet high.

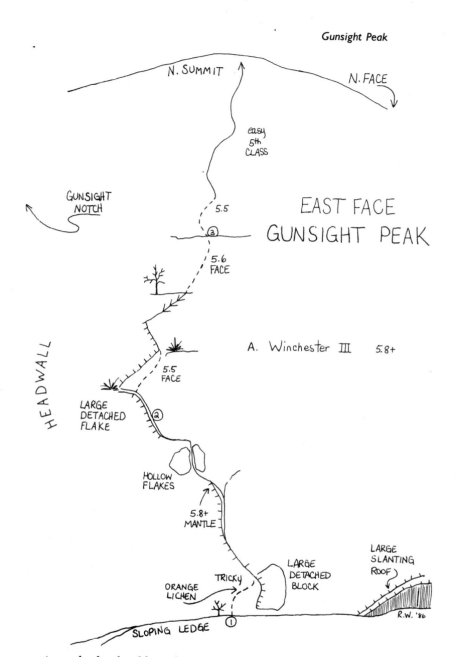

Ascend talus boulders above the tarn to the base of the headwall. Third class 200 feet up clean light gray slabs and benches that form an apron. Just right of the plumb line from the summit is a large detached block; orange lichen grows on the wall nearby.

Pitch 1: From the rope-up spot face climb up to a shallow corner above the large detached block. Continue up steep rock to a small dihedral. A difficult mantle (crux) leads up and left to a series of flakes. Climb up on good holds to another groove formed by a large block that is separated from the wall, belay 150 feet.

Pitch 2: Continue up to the top of a large detached flake to an ugly, dirty roof. Skirt the roof by face climbing the wall on the right. Sharp-edged holds abound. Continue up grooves for 150 feet, past a small dead tree, to a belay ledge.

Pitch 3: Climb over short cliffs and blocks on easier ground for 150 feet to the summit ridge. To descend, walk off McCormick Ridge to the northeast until it is possible to descend to the tarn.

South Summit—Northeast Face

Challenging third-class friction slabs, clean and crystalline, offer the soloist many opportunities to reach the top. To descend, climb down the north ridge to the notch or walk off the east ridge.

North Face

This 800-foot face appears quite dramatic from Mount Roothaan and Chimney Rock Trail #256.

Approach from the Crest via Horton Ridge access to Mount Roothaan. Once the north face is in view, traverse the southwestern flanks of Mount Roothaan to a notch in the ridge between the two peaks (Mount Roothaan and Gunsight Peak). At the notch it is possible to scramble into the basin formed by the north face cirque. An alternative approach may be from Chimney Rock Trail #256 from the east side. Ascend the trail to the ridge crest where Chimney Creek and West Branch Creek are separated. Cut cross-country over slabs and boulder fields into the West Branch basin (Gunsight, north face cirque).

Route Descriptions

A. BERGMAN/MILLER   III, 5.8/A2

On the left central portion of the north face is a chimney/dike that ascends to the highest portion of the face. Bergman and Miller descended the upper 200 feet of the route by rappel to inspect its possibilities. They then descended into the north face cirque and proceeded to climb the dirty and sometimes wet groove. Very little is known about the route, and it

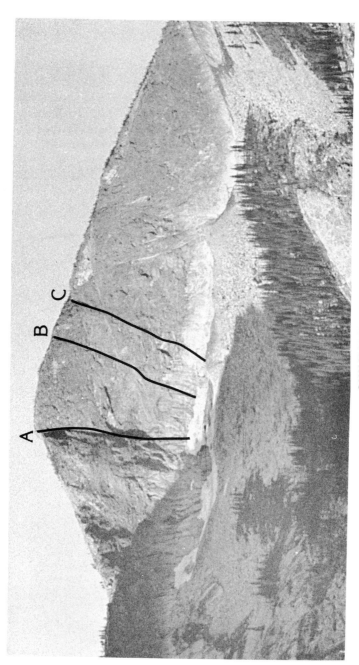

GUNSIGHT PEAK
North Face

A. Bergman/Miller Route   B. Roskelley/Castle Route   C. Oka/Bates Route (photo, Joe Bensen)

has never been climbed since. Pitons may still be required to secure belays.

B. ROSKELLEY/CASTLE   III, 5.9/AI (R)

This was the second route established on the north face. The route follows the next major weakness on the face to the right of the main chimney system. With a resemblance to route A (Bergman/Miller), this chimney/dike is more than five pitches in length, and the route does not protect well. John Roskelley led the whole route and sometimes encountered several unprotectable down-sloping slabs that were devoid of cracks. This climb has never been repeated. More information and details are unavailable.

C. OKA/BATES   III, 5.8

A third chimney/dike system splits the right wall several hundred feet west of the Roskelley/Castle route. This climb is approximately four pitches in length, with climbing similar to that found on routes A and B; it is, however, somewhat easier. There is no evidence of a second ascent. More information is unavailable.

6
Mount Roothaan
7326 ft. (2232 m)

Map: USGS Mt. Roothaan Quad 7.5 minute series

Second highest peak in the group covered in this guide, Mount Roothaan is a popular viewpoint for the casual summer hiker. Three ridges intersect at its summit to give it a triangular shape.

The south ridge is the crest divide and extends to Gunsight Peak. The west slope of the south ridge is gentle and descends toward Priest Lake, making Roothaan's summit easily attainable. The eastern side drops to the Chimney Creek drainage more dramatically and forms part of the east face. The northeast ridge extends to Chimney Rock and is the crest divide to the north. This ridge forms part of what is known as the Roothaan Cirque and offers many technical climbing possibilities, most of which have been ignored in favor of the main climbing attraction, Chimney Rock. The ridge itself is a thin vertical wall of granite over three hundred feet high and extends for a half mile. Chimney Rock was part of this ridge, but glaciation cut a deep gash in the ridge, leaving it as a solitary tower.

Access

The Horton Creek road that climbs to the top of Horton Ridge provides the best access. This road starts on the west side of the Selkirk Crest (Priest Lake side). An old fire lookout used to stand on a vantage point where the road ends. From there a moderately difficult hiking trail follows the southwestern flank of the northwestern ridge for about two miles to a notch a quarter mile short of the summit.

The northwest ridge drops steeply to form the Roothaan Cirque, but a rough climber's path provides access to the lower basin and the west face of Chimney Rock. This route is still used by many Spokane climbers visiting from the Priest Lake side.

Roothaan Cirque Route Descriptions

Northwest Face

A. NORTH NOSE I, 5.8

The north ridge of the Roothaan Cirque terminates at the notch that separates Chimney Rock from the rest of the cirque. At the end of the cirque ridge on the west side is a line that ascends through the flakes and blocks to the top. Start this one-pitch climb by scrambling up easy slabs until a secure belay is possible. Climb flakes and blocks up steep rock to the ridge crest.

B. GREAT CHIMNEY I, 5.6 (Not Shown)

The west side of the cirque ridge continues to offer climbing possibilities as it extends up to Mount Roothaan. About midway along the ridge is a long, parallel-sided chimney that splits the wall. Ascend this moderately difficult chimney and pass a troublesome chockstone. Little is known about this line and it has received few ascents.

East Face

A. NOTCHOS I, 5.8

On the east side of the north ridge of the Roothaan Cirque is a prominent notch between the Cirque Prow and Chimney Rock. Notchos ascends a line directly to the top of the notch from the bottom of the east face (right side).

Pitch 1: Ascend a slightly right-sloping flake system to a prominent ledge with a pine tree, then belay.

Pitch 2: Climb straight up, following a flake system. Strenuous lie-backs are abbreviated with ledges on which the climber can rest. Belay at top of the notch.

B. BLACK CRACK I, 5.8

This climb follows flakes and ledge systems on the left side of the notch (east face) to an obvious black crack that is the finish of the climb.

Pitch 1: Climb a flake to a ledge 8 inches wide and 15 feet long. Move right and face climb to a larger flake that is widely detached from the wall. From the top of the flake, climb easy ground past a left-slanting dead tree and up to a large live tree for the belay.

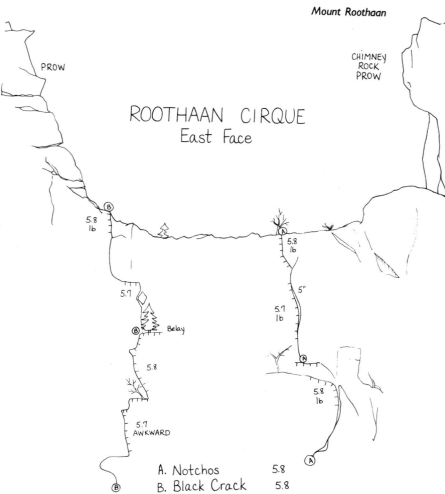

Pitch 2: A diamond-shaped, man-sized block must be passed to gain the upper black crack. Jam and lie-back to the top of the notch.

Descents

From the top of the notch between the north ridge of Roothaan Cirque and Chimney Rock, scramble around the northeast face of Chimney Rock to return to the base of the east face. Or rappel from the base of Magnum Force, Prow Ledge (150 feet) to base of East Face of Chimney Rock.

From the top of the north ridge (Roothaan Cirque), scramble south along the ridge until it is possible to down climb a small notch in the ridge near the main peak of Mount Roothaan.

7
Chimney Rock
7124 ft. (2171 m)

Map: USGS Mt. Roothaan Quad
7.5 minute series

Left by the glaciers to stand alone, Chimney Rock is sometimes referred to as the "Lightning Rod" of northern Idaho. This solitary summit was the first peak in the Selkirks to draw the climber's attention and is still a prized goal of many aspiring rock climbers from surrounding areas. Its isolated summit demands respect and requires some technical proficiency to scale by its easiest route.

Located a short distance northeast of Mount Roothaan, Chimney Rock is actually a disconnected portion of the Roothaan Cirque. It may be viewed from Priest Lake in the west or from the upper Pack River road on the east side. This granite tower is triangular in shape with the east and west faces meeting on the south edge to form a thin prow; the north face is the hypotenuse of the triangle. Littered with blocks of rubble, the summit is flat and exposed. At the base of the rock are large boulder fields (talus) on the east and west sides. These are the results of nature's destructive forces of erosion, breaking down the tower's outer layers.

The west face, the first face to be climbed, is about 350 feet high, with numerous flake/crack systems splitting it vertically. The rock on this side appears more shattered and blocky than on the other faces, and it is partially covered with lichens.

The east face looks more intimidating than the west face, since at 450 feet it is 100 feet higher and overhangs about 15 feet at the top. The rock on the east side is cleaner and more compact, with cracks formed by a proliferation of exfoliating flakes. The granite here is lighter in color and is extremely hard and crystalline, a condition that is generally excellent for free climbing.

The north face is dark and foreboding. Many crack lines lead to the steep overhanging summit, but black lichens prefer this exposure and tenaciously cling to the rough rock.

Protection

The rock is generally sound and protects well with a standard rack of chocks and nuts. Many of the cracks are parallel-sided, however, requiring Friends or cam devices. Fixed protection (bolts/pitons) may be encountered on some routes and rappel stations; please maintain them and leave them in place.

Some of the hard free climbs on the east face ascend thin, parallel-sided cracks that can be protected only by the new "Three Cam Units" (TCU's). Please do not use pitons on established routes that have been ascended by using "clean" methods of protection.

Historical Events

The summer of 1933 saw the first attempt by anyone to scale Chimney Rock. Lack of proper equipment and experience thwarted the pioneer party's attempt. John Carey returned the following summer with three other Seattle climbers, Mart Chamberlain, Fred Theime, and Byron Ward, to complete a successful ascent of the west face. They scouted the line of least resistance, which has since become the standard ascent route with a rating of 5.3 (route E in this section).

In 1935, John Boothe climbed the west face alone, following the same route used by the first ascent party. Early one summer morning, Boothe hitched a ride from his parent's cabin on Priest Lake to the south fork of Indian Creek. Carrying only a light jacket and snack, he scrambled through untracked wilderness, climbed the granite tower, and descended before dark. This was a remarkable achievement for the time. He worried not about the climb, but whether or not his tennis shoes would hold together long enough for the rough descent.

No new routes were climbed until 1959, when Ed Cooper and Don Bergman climbed the northeast face. This steep face required much direct aid, but has since been free climbed.

The next major feature to be climbed was the 450-foot vertical east face. This was accomplished in 1961, following an aborted attempt the preceding year. Ed Cooper and Dave Hiser completed the climb using some aid on the upper section of the route. This route was free climbed in 1972 by John Roskelley and Chris Kopczynski from Spokane. It has since become a classic and is the easiest route to the summit on the east face. For a description, see route K (Cooper-Hiser) in the East Face section of this chapter.

Not until 1968 was another route established, when Fred Beckey and Jerry Fuller climbed the South Nose, the thin prow that forms a knife edge. Beckey described the nose, as "being so thin it shakes."

With all the major faces climbed, Chimney Rock saw the beginning of a new era as another generation of climbers explored its features. Other major lines were opened by Kopczynski and Roskelley, who dominated the scene until the early 1970s. At this time free climbing trends found their way to the Selkirks and became the norm, with standards constantly rising. Countless first ascents await the adventurous; Chimney Rock is far from being climbed out.

Access

From the west (Priest Lake) side, ascend the Horton Creek road. At the end of the road, which is rough and steep (high-clearance or four-wheel-drive vehicles are suggested), is an adequate parking area near the site of the old lookout tower. Follow the well-traveled trail heading east up the ridge toward Mount Roothaan. After two miles of moderate hiking, you will reach a notch in the northwest ridge of Mount Roothaan. Here a rough climber's path descends the steep, broken north face into the basin formed by the Roothaan Cirque. This route takes one to two hours from the parking area.

Access from the east (Pack River) side has been improved by a group of local hikers and climbers who adopted old trail #256 and rerouted a portion of it. Approach via the Pack River road to the West Branch/Chimney Rock road. Follow the West Branch road and take the left fork as you cross Pack River. Stay right at all subsequent major intersections and follow the most traveled route 2.5 miles to the trailhead. A water bar discourages further vehicle travel and adequate parking is available at this point. Here, walk the upper road which follows Chimney Creek for about a half mile. When it is possible to cross the creek on an old wooden (log) bridge, start ascending skid/fire roads that switch back up a ridge separating the Chimney Creek and West Fork drainages. Continue up the path past blazes and cairns to a slabby ridge crest. Stay on the ridge crest until it is possible to traverse the east fact of Mount Roothaan on a natural bench that climbs at a gradual grade to the base of the east face of Chimney Rock. A climber's path skirts the base of the north face, giving access to and from the east and west faces. This route is 2.5 miles in length and can be walked in one to two hours.

Camping

The west side of Chimney Rock offers the nicest camping spots. There are established sites, but many areas are suitable. Water is present from springs even in late summer after a dry year. In late summer, however, no water is available at the base of the east face. Chimney Creek may be the last source when approaching from this side.

Several nice car campgrounds are located along the shoreline of Priest Lake. Indian Creek is the closest to the actual Horton Creek turn-off.

Route Descriptions

West Face

A.   SANCHO'S   II, 5.9

The left side of the west face offers numerous routes. Sancho's start is in grooves that lead to a small tree. From here it works up the northwest corner to later join route E (Standard Route) at the second rappel station.

Pitch 1: At the tree, climb a left-sloping groove to a right-facing corner, lie-back and jam to a roomy ledge (rappel station).

Pitch 2: Move to the left end of the ledge and climb a curving flake, 4″ protection helpful here. At the flake's end move right to another lie-back flake and continue up to the next belay on top of large blocks.

Pitch 3: Move left to easier ground, then climb over large blocks.

B.　SANCHO'S DIRECT　II, 5.10b (R)

At the second belay stance of route A (Sancho's), climb directly up thin cracks to same belay point for the third pitch on the regular route. Protection is difficult to place.

C.　TWIN CRACKS　I, 5.10a

This one-pitch climb, which looks deceptively appealing, begins on the left wall of a very clean open book, directly below the last rappel station (rock spike with slings). The unwary climber may be drawn onto a gently overhanging wall with two cracks devoid of holds. An exercise in off-hand and opposition technique lands one on the welcome flat ledge shared by route A (Sancho's), Pitch 2.

CC.　WEST SIDE GIRLS　I, 5.10a (X)

Confront difficulties directly by ascending the clean open book formation at the base of the Rappel Chimney. This dihedral leads to the same belay/rappel station for route D (Rappel Chimney). The protection is thin and difficult to place.

D.　RAPPEL CHIMNEY　II, 5.6

Although sharing the name with the descent route, it does not follow the line your ropes do on rappel. Keep moving right as difficulties increase. Follow the line of least resistance up grooves and flakes until you are into the chimney proper. Climb up toward the notch (rappel station) on the northwest shoulder.

Pitch 1: Follow grooves up and right of the blank open book below last rappel station. When level with anchors, traverse left to belay.

Pitch 2: Belay from rappel anchors, traverse out right to grooves leading up to large flakes, halfway up this pitch, step left into a chimney that leads to the next ledge. There are fixed belay/rappel anchors.

Pitch 3: Move left around corner from belay to easy fourth-class climbing over large blocks to summit.

RAPPEL CHIMNEY VARIATION　5.7

At the second belay (slings on spike), climb corner with jam crack to triangular ceiling block. Skirt block to the right and continue up and into chimney which leads to third belay on normal route.

RAPPEL CHIMNEY VARIATION 5.7

At the second belay, climb directly toward the main chimney via a 5.7 handcrack. At the end of the crack, step up and right to main chimney.

E. WEST FACE OR STANDARD ROUTE   II, 5.3

Thirty to forty feet right of route D (Rappel Chimney), the grooves on the face ascend at an easier angle. Follow the line of least resistance up grooves and behind blocks. This was the route the first ascent party followed in 1934.

Pitch 1: Scramble up easy grooves to a small tree near large blocks. A fixed pin marks the belay.

Pitch 2: Continue up and left in grooves with cracks to larger flakes, behind which one can climb. The next belay is not obvious, but there are many cracks to use for protection.

Pitch 3: Climb up and left to the northwest shoulder rappel station.

Pitch 4: Step around the left side of the northwest shoulder. Scramble up blocks to the top.

F. WEST FACE DIRECT   II, 5.9–

Fourth-class to the base of the open book in the middle of the face. During wet years the open book is often wet from a seep.

Pitch 1: Ascend the corner (off-width, 5") to a spacious ledge shared by a dead tree. Halfway up the corner, watch for a small crack on left wall. It takes nuts well.

Pitch 2: From belay move past a tree to climb cracks and blocks to the next groove/flake system on the left, which brings you to the top.

G. STICKY FINGERS   II, 5.10d (R)

This high-quality route is a less distinct crack system that begins to the right of a large loose flake near the start of West Face Direct (route F). A thin zigzag crack characterizes the line.

Pitch 1: Climb up and over a loose flake (poor protection up to and past the loose flake), follow a crack system to a belay at the ledge with the live tree.

Pitch 2: A continuous short, thin section is the crux. At the large block move left to easy climbing on shelves with loose rubble for the belay.

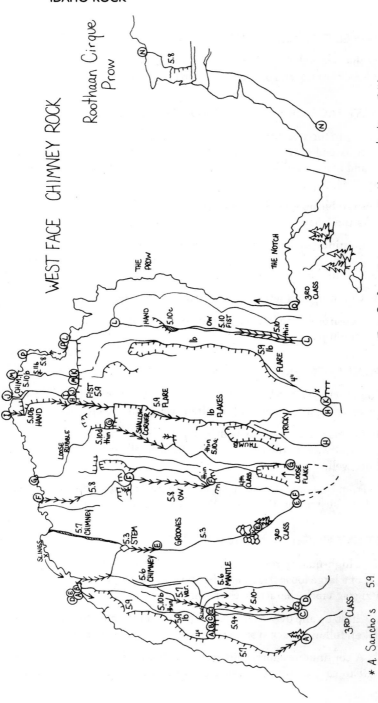

WEST FACE CHIMNEY ROCK

Roothaan Cirque Prow

* A. Sancho's 5.9
B. Sancho's Direct 5.10b(R)*
C. Twin Cracks 5.10a
CC. West Side Girls 5.10a
* D. Barrel Chimney 5.6/5.7
E. West Face Route 5.3
F. West Face Direct 5.9-
* G. Sticky Fingers 5.10d(R)
H. Scuffin-Up 5.9
* I. Fun Roof 5.3
J. Air Time 5.9-
* K. It Ain't Hay 5.10d(R)
L. Bera's Breeze 5.9
* M. Youranalysis 5.11b
N. North Nose 5.8
* O. Lord Greystoke 5.11b
P. South Nose Exit 5.8/A0 or 5.9

78

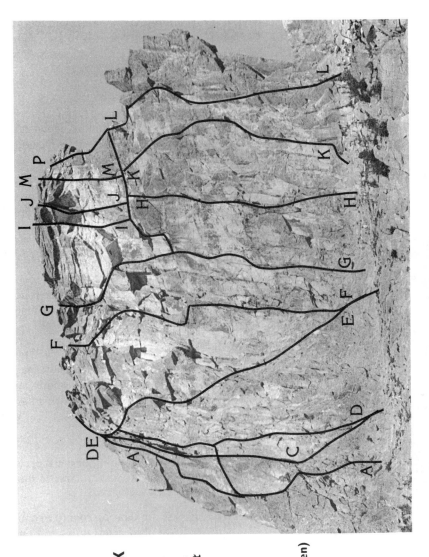

CHIMNEY ROCK
West Face

A. Sancho's
C. Twin Cracks
D. Rappel Chimney
E. West Face Route
F. West Face Direct
G. Sticky Fingers
H. Scuffin-Up
I. Fun Roof
J. Air Time
K. It Ain't Hay
L. Berg's Breeze
M. Youranalysis
P. South Nose exit
(photo, Joe Bensen)

Pitch 3: A short moderate pitch leads to summit via the loose and blocky line of least resistance on the left. An alternative finish is to step right around some big blocks and finish on route I (Fun Roof) or traverse off to the South Nose Exit.

H.   SCUFFIN-UP   II, 5.9

Scuffin-Up is the free version of the old aid climb, Broken Thumb. A large detached flake that looks like a thumb marks the line. However, several variations to the start (right of the thumb) are possible. Devious route finding may be involved to avoid unprotectable wide cracks.

Pitch 1: After the main crack system is gained, moderate lie-backing leads to a slightly overhanging slot. Scuff on up to a large ledge, directly below a roof split by two crack systems. At end of long pitch, belay from a roomy ledge.

Pitch 2: Go right to the South Nose Exit for an easier finish.

I.   FUN ROOF   I, 5.10b

Follow an open book to a horizontal roof that is directly above route H (Scuffin-Up). Undercling/jam the roof and gain upper crack by primate acrobatics. Strenuous and well protected with Friends.

J.   AIR TIME   I, 5.10b (R)

By following a line to the right of the Fun Roof corner, an alternate exit crack splits the roof. Right of the Fun Roof corner is a bomb-bay chimney. Sometimes called a 5.9 chimney with 5.11 exposure, this flaring slot is hard to protect.

K.   IT AIN'T HAY   II, 5.9

A popular route which involves several challenging lie-back problems, this climb follows a right-slanting crack system that flares to four inches at an easy roof (undercling to a lie-back).

Pitch 1: Follow the flake/crack system up past the slanting roof to a semi-detached paddle-shaped flake, then climb the thin crack to its end and move left to easy climbing on ledges and a roomy belay; exit via South Nose Route.

L.   BERG'S BREEZE   II, 5.10c (R)

A steep, shallow open book starts the climb that is farthest right on the face. From a certain vantage point, it is possible to see light through the whole Prow. Magnum Force is the climb that ascends the same crack system on the east face.

Pitch 1: Difficulties begin close to the ground, where a tight open book with a very thin crack must be chimneyed to gain the off-width flake/ crack above. Continue up by fist jamming/lie-backing or by off-width technique to a steep alcove. Loose rocks under the roof must be passed. Hand cracks of varying sizes lead through the roofs overhead. Belay on a roomy ledge (west side window).

Pitch 2: Next pitch can be Fun Roof, Youranalysis, Air Time or the South Nose Exit. A steep continuous line, this climb demands a variety of crack techniques.

M.   YOURANALYSIS   I, 5.11b

The next crack to the right of Air Time is a small dihedral that is split by a finger crack that goes over a bulge. Climb through the crack to the roof overhead.

East Face

A.   DIRTY HARRY'S REVENGE   I, 5.9

A one-pitch climb, this line follows challenging, steep lie-back flakes to the roomy ledge below the Prow. Scramble up a left-sloping third-class ledge to its end. A fixed pin marks belay. Move up and slightly right on face holds that give access to the crack system. Follow flakes and hand cracks to ledge at the notch.

B.   LORD GREYSTOKE   I, 5.11b

Accessible from the roomy ledge at the base of the Prow, this striking line catches the eye. It is gently overhanging, varies in size from thin fingers to thin hands, and demands your attention immediately. At the end of the forty-foot crack and after the major difficulties, a 5.10 mantle is a welcome relief. Rappel bolts are in place.

C.   SUDDEN IMPACT   I, 5.11b

Climb the direct line to route D (Magnum Force) and prow ledge. Follow a hand crack up to a shelf with a forked dead tree. Stem and lie-back the thin corner crack on the right. This leads directly to the rappel anchors. Fixed pins protect the strenuous and technical crux.

D.   MAGNUM FORCE   II, 5.10b

Twenty feet to the right of route B (Lord Greystoke), the steep white granite wall is split by a classic lie-back crack formed by a sharp-edged flake. Although the climb is not technical, its continuous nature makes it strenuous.

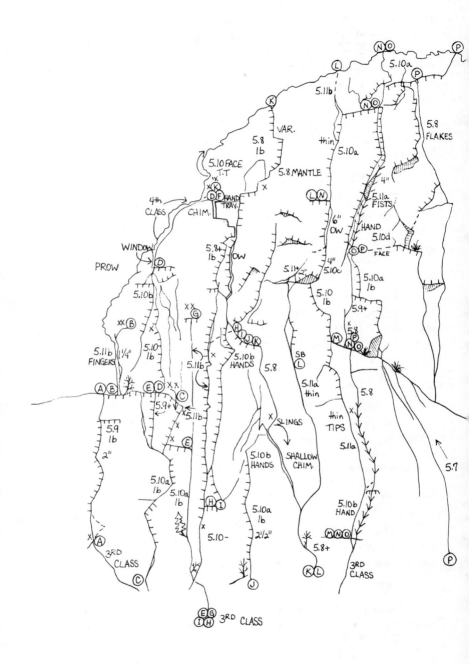

EAST/NORTH FACE CHIMNEY ROCK

* A. Dirty Harry's Revenge   5.9
* B. Lord Greystoke   5.11b
* C. Sudden Impact   5.11b
* D. Magnum Force   5.10b
* E. Wayward Son   5.10a
* F. South Nose Exit   5.8/AO or 5.9
* G. Kimmie   5.11c
* H. Yahoody   5.11b
* I. East Face Direct   5.10b
  * J. Canary Legs   5.10b
  * K. Cooper - Hiser   5.9-
  * L. Tsunami   5.11d (R)
  * M. Illusions   5.11a
  * N. Free Friends   5.10c
  * O. Eye of the Tiger   5.11a
  P. N.E. Face   5.10d (R)
  * Q. Graymatter   5.11c
  R. Clear Spot   5.8

Pitch 1: Follow the crack. At mid-height, the two old bolts near the 5-inch crack are a welcome alternative to protecting it. Continue up to a rest behind a block, then move left on good holds to gain easier ground up and left. Belay from the "window" (a large detached block you can see behind to the west face).

Pitch 2: Fourth-class climb up easier terrain leads to the South Nose finish.

E.   WAYWARD SON   I, 5.10a

This climb connects two crack systems and ends below route D (Magnum Force). It avoids the difficulties encountered at the top of route C (Sudden Impact).

Start at the same belay as routes H and I (Yahoody and East Face Direct). Climb a corner with a small juniper tree and continue up a steep fingertip lie-back crack to a ledge. At the ledge, traverse left and step down to another shelf with the forked dead tree. Climb the left corner crack formed by a block against the main wall.

F.   SOUTH NOSE EXIT   I, 5.8/A0 or 5.9

From a belay atop a large detached block, go up an easy slab that slopes down and to the east until the wall becomes vertical. A fixed pin and bolt protect thin, tricky moves out left onto the prow. Usually a tension traverse is used from the bolt to gain easier but overhanging blocks to the summit. Free, the moves past the bolt are at least 5.9.

G.   KIMMIE   II, 5.11c

Named for a lost friend, this climb continues up the crack system on which route E (Wayward Son) begins. From the belay shared by routes E, H, and I (Wayward Son, Yahoody and East Face Direct), climb Wayward Son past the first ledge and continue up 140 feet, following a steep thin crack until it fades. Fixed rappel anchors are in place.

H.   YAHOODY   II, 5.11b

This was the first 5.11 route on Chimney Rock and is still considered to be one of the most challenging. An exercise in hands, thin fingers, off-hands, fist, and off-width, this climb may test your full range of skills. After two pitches, traverse right to join the second belay stance for route K (Cooper-Hiser).

Pitch 1: Climb up a ramp/flake system to a small live tree, belay.

Pitch 2: A short tricky face pitch leads to the main crack system and a small ledge belay station.

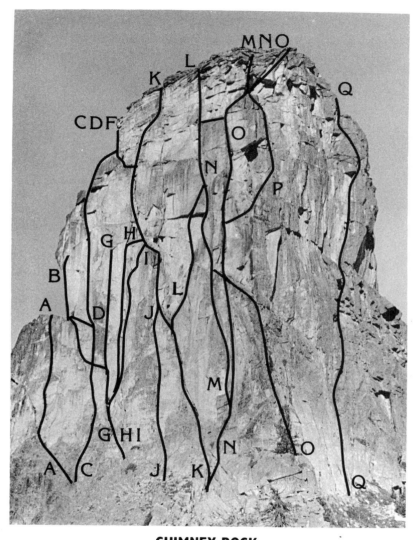

CHIMNEY ROCK
East and North Faces (N.E. Face)

A. Dirty Harry's Revenge
B. Lord Greystoke
C. Sudden Impact
D. Magnum Force
F. South Nose exit
G. Kimmie
H. Yahoody
I. East Face Direct
J. Canary Legs
K. Cooper-Hiser
L. Tsunami
M. Illusions
N. Free Friends
O. Eye of the Tiger
P. N.E. Face
Q. Graymatter

Rod Gibbons on Cooper-Hiser, ▲
Chimney Rock (photo, Joe Bensen)

Pitch 3: Follow the plumb line straight up through two small roofs until an off-width forces you to the right, where you will find easier ground and the sloping ledge belay stance of Cooper-Hiser. Continue up Cooper-Hiser or rappel off.

I. EAST FACE DIRECT II, 5.10b

This climb ascends a slightly easier crack system to the right of route H (Yahoody).

Pitch 1: Start at the same belay used for the first pitch on Yahoody.

Pitch 2: Ascend the same tricky face pitch to the next small belay ledge.

Pitch 3: At the belay ledge, follow the right-hand crack. This is formed by a flake that angles up and right to a sharp point (shark fin). At the point of the flake, climb to a small ledge rest and traverse right to the Cooper-Hiser belay ledge.

J. CANARY LEGS   I, 5.10b

This challenging crack may be lie-backed and jammed for 75 feet to a thin traverse right (crux) to join route K (Cooper-Hiser) at the old slings midway up the first pitch. Begin 15 feet left of Cooper-Hiser and follow the plumb line until forced right. Rappel or continue on Cooper-Hiser.

K. COOPER-HISER   III, 5.9−

The first route to be climbed on the east side was Cooper-Hiser, and it required aid. Now the route is a classic free climb, with excellent protection cracks. It ascends a line that begins in the middle of the face and gradually works up and left.

Pitch 1: Scramble to a groove that leans left and has a small dead tree clinging to it. Climb past tree (awkward) to a large groove. At the old rappel slings, climb up and right past an old ring piton into some steep hand cracks that are part of large blocks inside a huge chimney. Finish on a sloping ledge.

Pitch 2: At the belay, hand-traverse left with plenty of exposure to a flake system that may be lie-backed and jammed to another ledge at the top of a large block. Go left on a ledge to a large detached block (chimney behind the block) and climb to the belay on the prow.

Pitch 3: From the belay on the prow, finish the climb via the South Nose Exit.

Pitch 3a: Variation finish right: From the top of the large lie-back block, climb up and right to a tricky mantle which leads to easier climbing directly above.

L.   TSUNAMI   III, 5.11d (R)

Tsunami is Japanese for tidal wave. To date this is the hardest climb on Chimney Rock. Start at the same belay for the start of route K (Cooper-Hiser). Instead of moving left into the chimney system, move right and follow a line that splits the middle of the route N (Free Friends) roof.

Pitch 1: Climb past the dead tree to where it is possible to move right and up on thin cracks and flakes to a hanging belay (TCU's offer the best protection for this pitch).

Pitch 2: Continue up hand cracks that flare to off-width before entering the crack that splits the roof. The roof crack (crux) is hand size. Follow the crack to its end and step right to Free Friends route.

Pitch 3: Finish directly through the roof straight overhead. This was the original A2 pitch of the old Yellow Jacket route and is unprotectable.

M.   ILLUSIONS   I, 5.11a

The next major crack system to the right (north) of Cooper-Hiser is characterized by two cracks. Illusions is the one on the left. Ascend a third-class ramp/gully to a ledge. Belay at ledge and take the left crack up to a small ledge rest. Continue up polished rock on thin fingertip holds (crux). After 45 feet of sustained difficulties, the crack widens. At the ledge, continue up Free Friends or move right to a large ledge and escape down third class ramps toward the northeast.

N.   FREE FRIENDS   III, 5.10c

Start at the same belay as for route M (Illusions), but this climb continues on to the summit and involves a variety of sustained steep-crack climbing techniques.

Pitch 1: From the belay, climb left (Illusions) crack to small ledge rest. Move right to an easier crack that ends at a large ledge.

Pitch 2: Move left to the end of the ledge and ascend a crack and a lie-back flake to a roof. At the roof, jam, undercling, and lie-back to gain the upper crack that widens to off-width. At end of the off-width, a welcome ledge offers a belay stance. Big Friends are necessary for the belay anchors.

Pitch 3: Above belay, the crack thins down to fingers and continues to a spacious ledge atop a large pinnacle (40 feet).

Pitch 4: From belay on top of the pinnacle, move right to gain a crack system that threads through overhanging blocks to the summit.

O.   EYE OF THE TIGER   III, 5.11a

The start of this climb shares the same belay as routes M and N (Illusions and Free Friends). At the top of the first pitch of Free Friends, continue straight up the right side of the large pinnacle overhead.

Pitch 1: From the large ledge at the base of the pinnacle, climb cracks to the top of a large block. At the top of the block, lie-back to Micro-Scuzzem ledge and belay.

Pitch 2: Continue up a steep corner to an awkward flare (crux). Here the edge of the flake is overhanging and difficult to pass. After a few minor body contortions, fist-jam the upper crack along the edge of the pinnacle. Belay at the top of the pinnacle.

Pitch 3: Exit straight up overhead via the last pitch of Free Friend or traverse up and right on easy ledges to summit.

P.   NORTHEAST FACE   III, 5.10d (R)

Third-class easy ramps on the lower northeast arete to the second belay for route N (Free Friends) or the base of the large pinnacle and join route O (Eye of the Tiger).

Pitch 1: Follow cracks past the block to Micro-Scuzzem ledge and belay.

Pitch 2: Face climb right from the belay (crux), climb up and right to the broken north face proper. Continue up easier cracks to a large ledge which is right of the large pinnacle and near the summit.

Pitch 3: Scramble up easy ledges to summit.

North Face

Q.   GRAYMATTER   III, 5.11c

For the most part, the north face is steep, dark, and dirty. However, on the right side is a leaning gray dihedral capped by a three-foot roof that is relatively clean of lichens. This climb is well worth doing, but it does require extra cautiousness because of the large loose block at the top of the first pitch.

Pitch 1: Ascend a grungy crack to a bush. Awkward moves will be necessary to gain another crack that skirts a small roof. Then pass a bush and huge loose block. Belay at the ledge and base of the large gray dihedral.

Pitch 2: A large loose block must be passed to gain the crack that splits the dihedral above. Below the roof, where many #2 Friends are helpful, the crack is most sustained (crux), but past the roof, easier slabs lead to an alcove on the left. Belay in an alcove.

Pitch 3: The hand crack on the left ascends directly to the summit right of the main summit roofs.

R. CLEAR SPOT   I, 5.8

This is a one-pitch climb that starts from the trail near the northwest corner where a smooth face meets broken blocks. Climb a corner past two small ledges. Then follow a double crack system to a small slanted ledge in an open book capped by a roof. Traverse left and move up on face holds until it is possible to climb right to Sancho's (West Face, route A) belay station (sling rappel station) with rock horn.

Descents

Rappeling the northwest shoulder is the normal way to descend. Rappel stations are maintained and fairly easy to locate.

A short rappel of 40 feet gets the climber from the summit to the shoulder and the top of West Face, route D (Rappel Chimney). Here a double rope rappel will get you far enough down to allow easy down climbing the rest of the way to the bottom of the west face.

Another rappel station is located on the shoulder halfway down and is used when descending with one rope. It is also a handy place for the last person to retrieve ropes from the Rappel Chimney when descending with two ropes. There are several cracks that may snag your ropes if you pull them down from the base of the chimney.

8
Seven Sisters

Map: USGS The Wigwams Quad 7.5 minute series

This group of summits is sometimes referred to as the Seven Sisters. All of these peaks have steep faces left by glaciation. All, however, have easy scramble routes to their summits.

Silver Dollar Peak

When viewed from the east, Silver Dollar Peak is not very impressive. However, it has three steep faces that are of interest to the mountaineer.

The peak is divided into quadrants by four ridge lines. The east ridge, which extends to the Pack River, is broad and gentle, and is covered with stunted alpine fir. The north ridge, a continuation of the Selkirk Crest divide, branches off the peak halfway up the north face dividing it into two separate cirques—northeast and northwest. The lower faces in the cirques are slabby and broken, but relatively easy to climb. The upper north face is also quite broken and blocky, with many route possibilities in the moderate range. The west ridge is a rugged knife edge, guarded by several large blocky gendarmes. This ridge separates the northwest and southwest faces. The south ridge is the backbone of the Crest divide. The west side of this ridge is very steep and offers many technical climbing possibilities. The east side of the south ridge is gentler, and is covered with alpine fir and strewn with boulders.

Access

The best access to Silver Dollar is via the Chimney Rock east face route (Pack River road to Chimney Rock road; see Chimney Rock, Access, page 74). From the Chimney Rock Cirque, follow the crest ridge north.

▼ Silver Dollar Peak (photo, Joe Bensen)

Hike and scramble cross-country to the main peak. Access to routes on the north and west faces is best obtained by traversing north from the saddle on the south ridge.

An alternate approach is to follow Chimney Creek until it is possible to traverse to the right on old logging skid roads that switch back and ascend the ridge that separates Chimney Creek and Thor Creek. When the roads end, bushwhack a short distance up the ridge to a slabby ridge crest. Continue to follow the ridge crest until it is possible to traverse north toward the saddle or notch in Silver Dollar's south ridge. This route is shorter and more direct, but requires some route-finding skills.

A. WEST RIDGE   II, 5.3
(Not shown)

To date, few climbing routes have been recorded on the steep faces of Silver Dollar Peak. The West Ridge, however, is a classic mountaineering route. Exposed, aesthetic, and technical enough to be interesting, this route is worth doing. The views of the Crest divide from the ridge are beautiful and unique.

Gain access to the west face of the peak by descending a notch or saddle in the south ridge. Traverse under the west face until it is possible to begin scrambling up the south side of the west ridge. Scramble up to the crest of the ridge and continue following the line of least resistance to the top (two to three pitches, rated 5.2 – 5.3). A lower, more direct start may be more interesting and technical. No information is available about this portion of the route.

The Twins

Many challenging slabs and steep, broken faces exist on the group of summits just north of Silver Dollar. The Beehive Lakes are nestled between the Twins on the east side. This area is one of the most easily accessible pristine wilderness settings along this part of the Crest.

Access

These summits are accessible from the Beehive Lakes. Ascend trail #279 to the lakes from the upper Pack River road. The trail, about three miles long, is steep and rocky, but it is usually well maintained.

Harrison Peak
7292 ft. (2222 m)

Map: USGS The Wigwams Quad
7.5 minute series

Harrison Peak dominates the ridge that separates the Pack River headwaters from the Myrtle Creek drainage. Pack River flows south, eventually draining into Pend Oreille Lake, and Myrtle Creek flows east to drain into the Kootenai River.

Harrison overlooks a pretty lake which shares the same name and is a popular fishing spot. Another triangular-shaped peak, it has two impressively steep rock faces and one timbered shoulder that descends toward the east.

The west face is only about 150 feet high but is overhanging and, when viewed from the south, suggests a beak-shaped profile. This face extends north along the crest toward Two Mouth Lakes. The south face is over 400 feet high and offers many climbing possibilities from easy slabs and corners to steep cracks. This face begins by intersecting the east shoulder and extends down a long ridge line to the west.

The rock is exfoliating granite, and the climbing is generally friction slabs, corners, and cracks formed by flakes that have detached from the main walls.

Protection

A standard rack of nuts and chocks works well. However, flaring and parallel-sided cracks may be found, so Friends and cam devices are helpful. Fixed pitons may be encountered on some routes.

Access

Follow the Pack River road. Park a quarter mile from its terminus. A sign and an old jeep road mark the trailhead for Harrison Lake trail #271. Walk the old jeep road to the lake. Skirt the south end of the lake by following fisherman's paths to the main lake outlet. Follow a faint climber's path, which is marked with surveyor's flagging, up the ridge east of the lake. At the crest of the ridge when the whole south face of Harrison Peak is visible, work your way through scrub alpine timber to a large boulder field. Traverse talus slope to the base of the south face. This route takes two hours—one hour from the parking area to the lake and one hour from the lake to the base of the south face.

Camping

Established campsites are located at Harrison Lake. Lake water should be treated for bacteria before drinking.

Route Descriptions

South Face

A. MISTAKEN IDENTITY   II, 5.8/AI

The south face of the peak extends west along a steep ridge which is characterized by a large blocky gendarme. Mistaken Identity has an obvious left-angling crack system that splits the gendarme.

Pitch 1: Follow a crack and a flake to just below the blocky overhanging face of the gendarme. Here an off-width crack splits the block at a left-hand angle. Belay at the alcove below the wide crack.

Pitch 2: Aid into overhanging slot. Scramble onto the ridge on the west side of the gendarme.

Descent: Walk off the ridge crest to the west until it is possible to circle back to the south face.

B. GENDARME EAST   I, 5.8

The right-hand edge of the gendarme forms a large dihedral that extends away from the main plane of the south face. To the right of the corner is a series of flakes that leads to the ridge crest.

Pitch 1: Climb a line up and to the right of the gendarme; then climb slabs and work left to the notch on the ridge.

Pitch 2: Jam an awkward crack just below the ridge crest (crux), and belay on the ridge.

Descent: Down climb the north side of the ridge and walk west and around the end of the ridge until the south face may be gained.

Southeast Buttress & South/West Faces

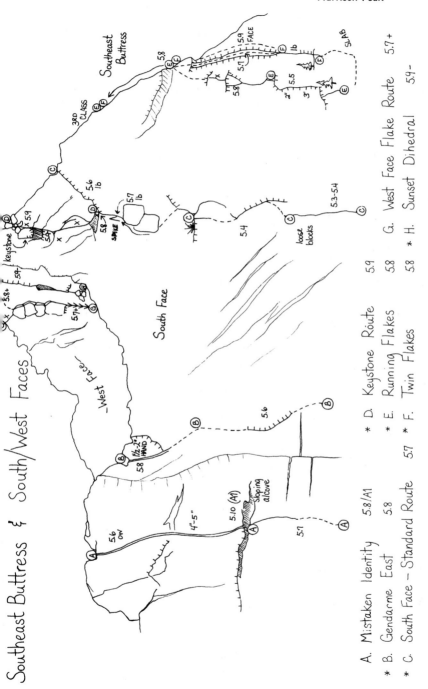

A. Mistaken Identity 5.8/A1

* B. Gendarme East 5.8

* C. South Face – Standard Route 5.7

* D. Keystone Route 5.9

* E. Running Flakes 5.8

* F. Twin Flakes 5.8

G. West Face Flake Route 5.7+

* H. Sunset Dihedral 5.9-

C. SOUTH FACE—STANDARD ROUTE   II, 5.7

This was the first technical rock climb on the peak. The three-pitch climb ascends directly up the flake systems that characterize the south face. Begin the climb by scrambling up toward the line descending directly below the summit. From the rope-up spot, many variations may be possible.

Pitch 1: Follow the line of least resistance (5.3/5.4) to a ledge strewn with loose rock. Belay and take care to not dislodge stones that may chop your rope.

Pitch 2: Move to the right across slabs to an obvious right-facing corner. Follow corners and cracks up to a roomy ledge shared by a prickly juniper bush; then belay.

Pitch 3: Move to the right from the belay until a crack and corner system may be gained. This system leads to the steep headwall and the summit. At the headwall, work to the right to a series of blocks that give access to a sharp corner system (crux). Lie-back up to a ledge. Lie-back one more corner. Easier ground then leads to the notch to the right of the summit. Belay at the notch. Scramble to the summit.

Descent: Scramble and walk off the east side of the peak until it is possible to drop down a steep trail that leads back around to the south face.

D. KEYSTONE ROUTE   II, 5.9

Follow route C (South Face—Standard Route) to just above the second lie-back on the third pitch. An obvious sloping ledge gives access to a direct line to the summit via the steep face. A fixed pin protects the awkward undercling moves to a crack that leads to an alcove and another fixed pin. Move to the left and continue up a crack to a square block (keystone). Under the keystone is an alcove rest. Climb a thin crack up and to the right of the keystone to gain larger cracks and broken blocks below the summit.

Southeast Buttress

E. RUNNING FLAKES   II, 5.8

Approximately 300 feet to the right (north) of route C (South Face—Standard Route) a trail with patches of bear grass gives way to a clean, scoured section of white and gray rock. The first thirty feet is broken by a small ledge and stubborn junipers.

▲ *Harrison Peak (photo, Joe Bensen)*

Pitch 1: Follow a small cleft forty feet from the base of the wall to a small ledge. Continue up a right-facing flake system for one hundred feet on very clean, granular rock. The belay platform is evident at the end of a 165-foot rope.

Pitch 2: Lead directly up and slightly to the left over a bulge and through a small system of dihedrals and face moves, good protection. Halfway up this pitch, climb through a small overhang to the "rock cornice" that makes up Harrison's southeastern skyline. Gain the belay stance directly under the right (northeast) edge of the cornice.

Pitch 3: From a white pocket, reach up and over a blind corner to the right. A bucket gives access to easy fifth-class mantles that will take you to the summit.

The descent is the same as for South Face—Standard Route.

F.   TWIN FLAKES   II, 5.8

Fifty feet to the right of route E (Running Flakes), scramble up forty feet and gain a stance and a sloping ledge with a juniper bush. The Twin Flakes route parallels Running Flakes.

Pitch 1: Climb directly up a left-facing flake and immediately stem right ten feet to a right-facing flake as it continues up for fifty feet; face climb to the left for fifteen feet on knobby, clean rock to the belay at a square ledge.

Pitch 2: From the belay that is the base of a double flake system, lie-back individual flakes or stem between them for one hundred feet to a steep face below the southeast arete and the rock cornice. Here the climb joins Running Flakes and shares the same belay below the rock cornice.

Pitch 3: Finish the climb by following blind moves out and to the right to a bucket hold that allows access to the arete.

The descent is the same as for Running Flakes.

TWIN FLAKES VARIATION   5.9

Pitch 1: Same as Twin Flakes route up first pitch.

Pitch 2: From the belay that is the base of the double flake system, face climb out to the right of the flakes. Protect by using the flake crack to the right of the double system.

Pitch 3: Continue up normal finish.

West Face

G.   WEST FACE FLAKE ROUTE   I, 5.7+

Approach the west face of the peak by walking around the west ridge to its base or by rappeling 150 feet off the summit. Looking at the peak's west face, near the summit is a prominent notch. The West Face Flake Route ascends a series of cracks, flakes, and blocks to a point that is just to the left of the notch. Follow a small dihedral with a crack up to a large detached flake. Mantle onto a sloping shelf, go up to and behind large flakes and blocks with a cave. Go left behind block or face climb right to the summit.

H.   SUNSET DIHEDRAL   I, 5.9−

Directly below the prominent notch in the summit is a clean open book that begins with an inverted V slot. Chimney and squeeze past the slot to gain access to the dihedral. A thin finger crack provides a chance for bomber protection and the stemming up the corner is classic and clean. Follow the dihedral to the summit.

Appendices

▲ *Author at Granite Point (photo, Joe Bensen)*

A
First Ascents*

Schweitzer Practice Rocks Routes

Name of Route	Rating	Name of Party	Date
Laceration	5.7	V. Lemley/R. Green	1979
Cave Crack	5.4	J. Bensen/T. Green	1980
Fern Crack	5.7	R. Green/J. Bensen	1980
Reptilian	5.7	R. Green/V. Lemley	1980
Shortcake	5.6	R. Green/J. Bensen	1980
Blind Man's Bluff	5.5	J. Bensen/R. Green	1980
Batso	5.8+	R. Green/J. Bensen	1981
Definitely Maybe	5.9	R. Green/J. Bensen	1981
Blindman's Bluff— Right Variation	5.8+	R. Green/J. Bensen	1981
East Face Direct	5.8/A2	V. Lemley/R. Green	1981
Stonemaster's Delight (FFA of E. Face Dir.)	5.10c	R. Green/R. Gibbons T. Green	1986
Ho-Di-Do	5.10a	R. Green/T. Green	1984
Ho-Di-Do—Exit Stage Right Variation (FFA)	5.10a	R. Green/T. Jensen	1985
Reptilian—In and Out Variation	5.8	M. Potucek	1985
Astro Monkey Roof (FFA)	5.10b	R. Green/R. Gibbons	1986
Gotch-Ya	5.10a	Unknown	1986
Muskrat Love	5.9	K. Birkinkamp/T. Rowe	1986
Metamorphosis (FFA)	5.10c	T. Jensen/G. Klein	1986

*Listed in chronological order. FA—First Ascent; FFA—First Free Ascent; FFS—First Free Solo; FWA—First Winter Ascent.

Laclede Rocks Routes

Name of Route	Rating	Name of Party	Date
Lower/East Side Cliff			
Jensen's Dihedral (FFA)	5.9	T. Jensen/G. Klein	1986
Buried Treasure	5.7	R. Green/T. Jensen K. Birkinkamp	1986
Sod-Buster	5.6	T. Jensen/G. Klein	1986
Lock Tight	5.10a	K. Birkinkamp	1986
Road Kill	5.11c	D. Fulton/D. Burns	1986
Upper and Lower Main Cliff			
The Dihedral (FFA)	5.9–	R. Green/J. Bensen	1982
(FFS)		D. Burns	1986
Organ Grinder (FFA)	5.10b	J. Bensen/R. Green	1983
Hang-Over	5.7	T. Applegate/G. Head	1985
Grungy Chimney (FFS)	5.5	K. Birkinkamp	1985
About Face (FFA)	5.10b	K. Birkinkamp/T. Applegate	1985
March of Dimes	5.8+	R. Green/V. Lemley	1985
Drag Queen	5.7	R. Green/T. Applegate K. Birkinkamp	1986
Double Trouble	5.8	T. Applegate/R. Green G. Klein	1986
Hornet's Nest	5.8–	R. Green/T. Applegate	1986
Chicken McNubbins (FFA)	5.10b	R. Green/R. Gibbons	1986
Schmutzig-Buchen	5.10/A0	T. Jensen/R. Green R. Gibbons	1986
Weasels Ripped My Flesh—Side 1 (FFA of Schmutzig-Buchen)	5.10d	D. Burns/D. Fulton	1986
Moonshadow	5.10/A0	R. Green/R. Gibbons	1986
Weasels Ripped My Flesh—Side 2 (FFA of Moonshadow)	5.11c	D. Burns/D. Fulton	1986
Psycho Killer (FFA)	5.11a	R. Green/K. Birkinkamp	1986

Laclede Rocks Cont'd.

Name of Route	Rating	Name of Party	Date
Orangutan	5.10b	K. Birkinkamp	1986
(FFS)			
Crap Shooter	5.10a	T. Applegate/R. Gibbons	1986
(FFA)		L. Peterman	
Donation	5.7	Unknown	
Hitchhiker	5.8−	T. Jensen/T. Applegate	1986
		R. Gibbons	
Three Friends	5.8−	R. Gibbons/T. Applegate	1986
		T. Jensen	
Poster Child (FA)	5.11c/A0	R. Green	1986
(FFA)	5.11c	L. Peterman	1986
Radioactive	5.10c	R. Green/R. Gibbons	1986
(FFA)			
Shook Me	5.10b	R. Green/R. Gibbons	1986
(FFA)		T. Applegate	

Utility Pole Buttress

New Sensations	5.9	R. Green/J. Bensen	1985
(FFA Right Finish)		T. Jensen	
Var. Dir. Finish	5.8	J. Bensen/R. Green	1985
		T. Jensen	

Blasted Right-of-Way

Railyard Blues	5.10/A0	R. Green/T. Jensen	1985
(FFA)	5.10c	R. Green/R. Gibbons	1986

Granite Point Routes

Little Wall (Flying Squirrel Buttress)

Beeline	5.5	M. Heumanm/T. Jensen	1982
Shoreline	5.7	M. Potucek/T. Jensen	1984
Waterline	5.8	M. Potucek/T. Jensen	1984
Mainline	5.10c	R. Green/J. Bensen	
(FFA)		T. Jensen	1985
Dir. Finish	5.10d	R. Green/T. Jensen	
(FFA)		C. Hecht/J. Bensen	1986
Beeline—110 Degrees			
Variation	5.10a	J. Bensen/R. Green	
(FFA)		T. Jensen	1985

Granite Point Routes Cont'd.

Name of Route	Rating	Name of Party	Date
Troll Tower			
Ogre Off-Width	5.9	T. Jensen/R. Green	1985
Foreboding Buttress			
Fear and Loathing	5.8	R. Green/V. Lemley	
		T. Green/T. Jensen	1984
Big Wall (Sunset Buttress)			
Fingerling	5.10c	D. Ming/J. Bensen	1982
(FFA)			
Dir. Fin.	5.10c	R. Green/T. Jensen	1986
(FFA)		K. Birkinkamp	
Reasonable Alternative	5.9	R. Green/T. Jensen	1986
Bombay Chimney 101	5.7	J. Bensen/C. Hecht	1986

Gunsight Peak Routes

East Face			
Winchester	5.8+	R. Green/R. Gibbons	1985
North Face			
Bergman/Miller	5.8/A2	D. Bergman/J. Miller	1962
Roskelley/Castle	5.9/A1	J. Roskelley/G. Castle	1969
Oka/Bates	5.8	G. Oka/H. Bates	1978
Roothaan Cirque Routes			
North Nose	5.8	C. Kopczynski	1968
(FFA)		C. Kopczynski	
Great Chimney	5.6	J. Roskelley	1968
(FFA)			
Notchos	5.8	R. Green/R. Gibbons	1986
		K. Birkinkamp	
Black Crack	5.8	T. Jensen/K. Birkinkamp	1986

Chimney Rock Routes

Name of Route	Rating	Name of Party	Date

West Face

Name of Route	Rating	Name of Party	Date
West Face (Standard Route)	5.3	J. Carey/B. Ward F. Theime/M. Chamberlain	1934
West Face (FFS)	5.3	J. Boothe	1935
West Face (FWA)	5.3	D. Kurtz/G. Johnson G. Stitcinger	1973
Rappel Chimney	5.6	Unknown	
Rappel Chimney (FFS)	5.6	J. Spearman	1971
Broken Thumb	5.7/A1	C. Kopczynski C. Kopczynski	1968
Scuffin-Up (FFA of Broken Thumb)	5.9	R. Bergner/T. Nephew	1974
West Face Direct	5.7/A2	C. Kopczynski J. Roskelley	1968
West Face Dir. (FFA)	5.9–	J. Jones/G. Silver	1972
West Face Dir. (FWA)	5.7/A2	W. Parks/C. Kopczynski	1973
It Won't Go	5.6/A2	C. Kopczynski C. Kopczynski	1968
Berg's Breeze (FFA of It Won't Go)	5.10c	R. Bergner/T. Nephew	1974
Sancho's (FFA)	5.9	J. Roskelley J. Roskelley/C. Kopczynski	1971
Boogie Jive	5.6/A2	J. Spearman/W. Parks	1972
It Ain't Hay (FFA of Boogie Jive)	5.9	T. Nephew/R. Bergner	1974
Twin Cracks (FFA)	5.10a	D. Sather/P. Stevenson	1979
Air Time (FFA)	5.10b	K. Momb/T. Ray	1979
Fun Roof (FFA)	5.10b	G. Oka/D. Burns H. Bates	1980
Sancho's Direct (FFA)	5.10b	G. Oka/H. Bates	1980

Chimney Rock Routes cont'd.

Name of Route	Rating	Name of Party	Date
Sticky Fingers (FFA)	5.10d	G. Oka/H: Bates T. Ray	1980
Twin Cracks—West Side Girls Variation (FFA)	5.10a	D. Burns/J. Purdy	1986
Youranalysis (FFA)	5.11b	D. Burns/J. Koopsen W. Rockafellow	1986

East Face

Name of Route	Rating	Name of Party	Date
Northeast Face	5.8/A2	D. Bergman/E. Cooper	1959
Northeast Face (FFA)	5.10d	D. Burns/M. Colby	1980
Northeast Arete (Var. N.E. Face 2nd pitch)	5.10d	D. Burns/J. Langdon T. Ray	1980
Eye of the Tiger (FFCont. Ascent N.E. Arete)	5.11a	D. Burns/W. Parks	1981
East Face	5.8/A1	E. Cooper/D. Hiser	1961
Cooper-Hiser (FFA of E. Face)	5.9−	C. Kopczynski J. Roskelley	1972
Cooper-Hiser Dir. Finish (FFA)	5.8	T. Nephew/R. Bergner W. Parks	1973
South Nose	5.7/A2	F. Beckey/J. Fuller	1968
Magnum Force (FFA of South Nose Rt.)	5.10b	J. Roskelley/T. Ray	1977
Yellow Jacket	5.7/A3	J. Roskelley/J. Spearman	1970
Free Friends (FFA of Yellow Jacket)	5.10c	D. Burns/G. Silver	1980
East Face Direct (FFA)	5.10b	R. Bergner/T. Nephew	1974
Canary Legs (FFA)	5.10b	R. Bergner/T. Nephew	1974
Yahoody (FFA)	5.11b	D. Burns/D. Burns	1980
Illusions (FFA)	5.11a	D. Burns/M. Colby	1981
Dirty Harry's Revenge	5.9	R. Green/R. Gibbons	1985
Lord Greystoke (FFA)	5.11b	M. McBirney/V. Lemley	1985

Chimney Rock Routes cont'd.

Name of Route	Rating	Name of Party	Date
Wayward Son (FFA)	5.10a	R. Green/R. Gibbons	1986
Sudden Impact (FFA)	5.11b	R. Green/D. Burns D. Fulton	1986
Kimmie (FFA)	5.11c	D. Burns/J. Koopsen	1986
Tsunami (FA)	5.11d	D. Burns/J. Koopsen	1986

North Face

Name of Route	Rating	Name of Party	Date
Graymatter (FFA)	5.11c	D. Burns/C. Hartshorn	1980
Clear Spot (FFA)	5.8	T. Applegate/G. Head	1985

Harrison Peak Routes

South Face

Name of Route	Rating	Name of Party	Date
South Face—Standard Route	5.7	Unknown	
Gendarme East	5.8	R. Green/T. Green	1981
Mistaken Identity	5.8/A1	J. Bensen M. Potucek/J. Judge	1981
Keystone Route (FFA)	5.9	R. Green/M. Kubiak K. Nystrom	1984

Southeast Buttress

Name of Route	Rating	Name of Party	Date
Running Flakes	5.8	M. Potucek	1982
Twin Flakes	5.8	M. Potucek	1983
Twin Flakes Variation (FFA)	5.9	M. Potucek	1983

West Face

Name of Route	Rating	Name of Party	Date
West Face Flake Route	5.7+	R. Green/T. Green	1981
Sunset Dihedral (FFA)	5.9−	R. Green/J. Bensen T. Green	1984

B

Comparison of Free Climbs
Crux Moves Used as Reference
Listed in Order of Difficulty

Face Climbs

Reptilian	5.7
Three Friends	5.8−
Hornet's Nest	5.8−
Clear Spot	5.8
Double Trouble	5.8
Oka/Bates	5.8
Batso	5.8+
South Nose	5.9
Definitely Maybe	5.9
Orangutan	5.10b
Chicken McNubbins	5.10b (compares with Pebbles, Peshastin)
Radioactive	5.10c
Northeast Face, Chimney Rock	5.10d
Tsunami (third pitch)	5.11b
Poster Child	5.11c

Chimneys/Off-Widths

West Face, Silver Dollar	5.3
West Face, Chimney Rock	5.3
Grungy Chimney	5.5
Shortcake	5.6
Great Chimney	5.6
Rappel Chimney	5.6
Bombay Chimney 101	5.7
West Face Flake, Harrison Peak	5.7+
Scuffin-Up	5.9
Ogre Off-Width	5.9
Twin Cracks—West Side Girls Variation	5.10a

Chimneys/Off-Widths Cont'd.

Fern Crack—Astro Monkey Roof Variation	5.10b
Air Time	5.10b
Berg's Breeze	5.10c
Eye of the Tiger	5.11a (compares with Twilight Zone, Yosemite)

Lie-Back/Stem Corners

Cave Crack	5.4
Sod-Buster	5.6
Donation	5.7
Hang-Over	5.7
Buried Treasure	5.7
South Face, Harrison Peak	5.7
Twin Flakes	5.8
Running Flakes	5.8
New Sensations	5.8
Black Crack	5.8
Notchos	5.8
March of Dimes	5.8+
The Dihedral	5.9–
West Face Direct	5.9–
Sunset Dihedral	5.9–
Cooper-Hiser	5.9– (compares with Central Pillar of Frenzy, Yosemite)
Sancho's	5.9
Jensen's Dihedral	5.9
It Ain't Hay	5.9
Dirty Harry's Revenge	5.9
Reasonable Alternative	5.9
Crap Shooter	5.10a
110 Degrees	5.10a
Wayward Son	5.10a
About Face	5.10b
Shook Me	5.10b
Organ Grinder	5.10b
Magnum Force	5.10b (compares with First Pitch of Outer Limits, Yosemite)
Metamorphosis	5.10c
Stonemaster's Delight	5.10c
Free Friends	5.10c (compares with Good Book, Yosemite)

Lie-Back/Stem Corners Cont'd.

Sticky Fingers	5.10d
Sudden Impact	5.11b
Road Kill	5.11c (unique)
Another Roof	5.12

Thin Cracks (up to 1.5")

Fern Crack	5.7
Reptilian—In and Out Variation	5.8
Fear and Loathing	5.8
Muskrat Love	5.9
Keystone Route	5.9
Ho-Di-Do	5.10a
Lock Tight	5.10a
Exit Stage Right	5.10a
Sancho's Direct	5.10b
Railyard Blues	5.10c (compares with Lunatic Fringe, Yosemite)
Fingerling	5.10c
Mainline	5.10d
Weasels Ripped My Flesh—Side 1	5.10d
Illusions	5.11a (compares with Butterfingers, Yosemite)
Psycho Killer	5.11a
Tsunami (1st pitch)	5.11a
Lord Greystoke	5.11b
Yahoody	5.11b
Kimmie	5.11c
Graymatter	5.11c (compares with Fourth Pitch Astroman, Yosemite)
Weasels Ripped My Flesh—Side 2	5.11c
Tsunami (2nd pitch)	5.11d

Hand/Fist Cracks (1.5" or wider)

Beeline	5.5
Blind Man's Bluff	5.5
Shoreline	5.7
Drag Queen	5.7
Laceration	5.7
Hitchhiker	5.8–
Gendarme East	5.8
Waterline	5.8
North Nose	5.8
Twin Cracks	5.10a
Canary Legs	5.10b
East Face Direct	5.10b
Fun Roof	5.10b
Youranalysis	5.11b (compares with Floatation, Leavenworth)

Index

About the Author

Randall Green has lived and climbed in the Sandpoint area for over ten years and has climbed more than seventy-five percent of the established technical climbing routes there, pioneering many. He has taught rock climbing skills to young people and adults since 1980 in conjunction with summer ski racing camps in Oregon. Currently he is teaching climbing and directing a mountain guide service in Sandpoint.

His climbing experience extends from many Grade V and Grade IV routes in the Cascades and Canada to several Grade VI routes in Yosemite. He has traveled throughout the western United States, climbing at several well-developed climbing parks, as well as at areas such as the Tetons, Devils Tower, and some of the sandstone towers of the Colorado and Utah deserts. He and his wife climbed in New Zealand in 1978.

Randall has coauthored two rock-climbing articles that have been published by *Rock and Ice* and *Climbing* magazines.